Ha! Ha!
Among the Trumpets

Ha! Ha!

Among the Trumpets

Sermons by

Martin H. Franzmann

CPH™
ST. LOUIS

Preface

The trumpet seems far too demonstrative an instrument to delight the likes of Martin Franzmann. He was a quiet, gentle man, not a brassy creature at all. Yet his writing is lively, as brilliant to the reader as any trumpet is to the hearer. Yes, he like trumpets, especially God's trumpet, "A trumpet none could silence or mistake."

With this reprint of Dr. Franzmann's book of sermons, a new audience, and perhaps some of the old who missed it the first time around, will have the opportunity to catch the fresh air of his clear proclamation of God's Word, a preaching that, it seems, time will not easily "silence or mistake."

For just over a year I joined the staff and students at Westfield House, Cambridge, for the weekly Pericope Seminar when Martin Franzmann conducted it. Here one could see the exegete-preacher at work, preparing for the weekly proclamation of the Word in its liturgical setting of the Divine Service. "The purpose of this seminar," he said by way of introduction, "is worship."

The seminar was memorable for many reasons. For some it was above all learning to ask the right questions of the text. That was the beginning of effective and faithful proclamation. "Never," he instructed, "allow the words 'OF COURSE' be used." That was how he confronted the danger of familiarity with the text. Memorable for us all were the regular "one-liners" of wisdom.

ON TEXTUAL PREACHING: "Without a text, you feel like Adam without your fig leaves."

Or who would forget the lecture on homiletics that featured the schoolboy's "spitball."

ON PREACHING AS A "SPITBALL": "First take a piece of paper. Masticate it. Then aim it—behind the ear. Sometimes a spitball is shot at the ceiling; that is not the kind we want."

ON GRIMNESS IN PREACHING: "There is a tendency today for preachers to feel that a joyful preaching is shallow. It must be existentially grim. Don't keep such a cold stove that the cats won't come to eat. It must have doxology. When you stop having doxology, you're not preaching."

ON PULPIT ORATORY: "What keeps a man from being a pulpit orator is being a pastor."

SERMON, SERMONETTE, OR WHAT? "Call a sermon a 'sermon'; don't avoid that and call it a 'meditation' or 'sermonette' or even 'brief sermon.' DARE TO SAY: 'I'm going to preach to you!'"

About his delivery one would not use that questionable expression that he "preached with power." The real power, he would prefer to say "authority," of his words was in their substance, not in their style; he trusted that they were God's words. There was in him no "tired elegance" nor "neurotic pulpit eloquence" (see his own Preface to the first edition). 'Yet, how can one overlook his style. For even his spoken words were based on that skill that he had mastered better than most—a mastery of the written word. "Write a lot," he encouraged. Then he would quote a German saying, "Write till you are free."

Even his titles are exceptional. Certainly the last one in this collection is brilliant. Here Franzmann retells the story, homily style as he called it, with the refrain, "And what happens then?" (See also the earlier use of the refrain, "The disciples failed." pp. 41ff.)

For those readers who are preachers another bit of Dr. Franzmann's advice would be appropriate: "In reading sermons (of other men), don't read any which you can imitate directly. God has placed you in that pulpit for that time, not to imitate a Mr. Big Preacher." Yet the wise preacher can still learn from this servant of the Word who would often twist the phrase "understand the Scripture" to say, "one must stand under the Word."

The quality of writing shows when its effectiveness endures; Franzmann's delivery of the message is as fresh today as ever. What could be more relevant for today than his warning about *Ersatz* hymnody (p. 95), more pointed than his identification of the "lurking paganism" in us (p. 87)? Where could one hear clearer gospel than the description of a battle won (p. 18) or of "the man who went home with only a word in his pocket" (pp. 104 ff.)? Every sermon ends on a note of "high doxology" in the declaration of the forgiving love of our Lord.

Ronald Feuerhahn

Contents

1

HA! HA! AMONG THE TRUMPETS

(Seminary Graduation)

*Rejoice evermore. Pray without ceasing. In everything give
thanks, for this is the will of God in Christ Jesus concerning you.*
1 THESSALONIANS 5:16-18

Nowhere in that jubilant and exuberant book, the Old Testament, is there such an expression of joyful wonder at the
creation of God as in the latter chapters of the Book of Job.
They are, as it were, an echo of God's own "Very good!" —
a reflection of the delight and love with which God Himself
embraces and sustains His handiwork (A. Weiser). And
in all these chapters, in all these pictures of beings fearfully
and wonderfully made, there is none quite like the picture
of the horse in his strength (39:19-25), the horse whose
neck is clothed with thunder, the glory of whose nostrils is
terrible, who paweth in the valley and rejoiceth in his strength,
who mocketh at fear, who swalloweth the ground with fear
and rage — "He saith among the trumpets, 'Ha! Ha!' "

God has made him a horse, a steed of war. He delights
in being a horse; he is glad to work like a horse and to fight
like a steed of war. He hears the trumpets of war, and he

cannot stand still at the sound of the trumpet; that trumpet is God's call to him to be what God has made him. And he greets that call with an equine Alleluia! He snuffs the air, and stamps the ground, and "saith among the trumpets, 'Ha! Ha!'"

Summoning us to such an Alleluia to God, who has shined out of darkness and created us anew in Christ Jesus, St. Paul bids us: "Rejoice evermore." He is bidding us enter with gusto, exuberance, and vigor upon the work that God has created us for, upon the works He Himself has before prepared that we should walk in them. The apostle is calling us to enter gladly, vigorously, and resolutely upon our ministry; he is calling us to a glad and resolute Ha! Ha! among the trumpets.

St. Paul is not summoning us to any easy, smiling optimism, to any easy and shallow exposure of our teeth. He is calling us to give heed to that which triumphs over death and gives us the victory. He is calling us to give ear to the trumpet call of God and to cry Ha! Ha! among the trumpets.

I. The Trumpets of God: "Rejoice evermore . . . for this is the will of God in Christ Jesus concerning you."

The trumpet of God has sounded — one long, sonorous arabesque of sound which broke upon the midnight air when the angels brought good tidings of great joy to shepherds, and all the hosts of heaven made melody when the glory of the Lord shone round about them, a trumpet call that rose with a swell and a surge as of the sound of many waters to rend the veil of the temple and to shake the earth to open all men's graves, when our Lord was crucified and rose again. And that trumpet call is for *us:* "This is the will of God in Christ Jesus concerning *you.*" This trumpet call bids you snuff that Easter air, that air from which our Lord, upon the cross,

4

has swept away all the dank and poisonous vapors of sin, all the miasma of mortality; it bids you scent that eternal air, and stamp that Easter-cloven ground, and to stand in triumph on your graves, and to cry Ha! Ha!

That blast reverberates through all the valleys of time and place, and all the trumpet calls that we shall hear in all our ministry are but echoes and repercussions of that one triumphant blast. We shall hear the trumpets of God. We shall hear the cutting rigor of the stern and deep-throated trumpet call to repentance: "Draw near to God, for He has drawn near to you! Turn ye, turn ye — turn from yourselves, and your sin, and your contorted revolt against your God. Repent, for the kingdom of heaven has drawn near!" And with it, at once, we shall hear the melody of mercy, the silver solace of the trumpet of the forgiveness of our God, that trumpet which breathes the cross and tells us, "It is finished," and spells out for us with every silver tone, "Thy sins be forgiven thee." Greet that trumpet in both its tones with resolute rejoicing. Say Ha! Ha! among these trumpets of God.

And with the sounding of these trumpets there is released also the eternal music, brave and resonant and pure, of love, the love which never faileth. It is the love of God that does not find but creates the object of its love — that love at work upon us, in us, and through us, to make our ministry a ministry like His who came to minister and give His life a ransom for many. Greet that trumpet call with a reckless self-giving love that rejoices to spend and be spent, and thus speak your Ha! Ha! to that trumpet of God.

You are entering the *Christian* ministry, and you shall hear the clear, succinct, and doubtless staccato call to confession: "Whosoever will confess me before men, him will I confess also before my Father which is in heaven." Our Lord Himself has promised us the Holy Spirit to enable us to answer this call, to say Ha! Ha! to this trumpet even though it may mean danger, even though it may mean death. And this Holy Spirit will enable us to do what *we* can never do: to confess the *truth*.

This Spirit of our God will give us ears to hear another trumpet tone: the pure and valid tones of the simplicity of truth, amid the whine and chatter of half-truths, twisted truths, and lies. We must greet that trumpet too with a brave Ha! Ha! And who is sufficient for that? But there is still another trumpet, resounding sonorous tones of strength: "Be strong in the Lord and in the power of His might. Put on the whole armor of God." And with that trumpet tone in our ears we know that we can resist the devil, and he will flee from us. One little word — "Jesus is Lord!" — can fell him; he will flee from us. You are to be confessing ministers: "We believe, teach, and confess!" Give ear to the marching beat of this trumpet of the power of the mastery of God's own might, and greet it with a bold Ha! Ha!

Our Lutheran confessors made their confession in the consciousness that they must all appear before the judgment throne of Christ; and we must all confess with the end in view, for confession is always an eschatological act. And so it is given to us to hear also the long crescendo of the horns of hope. And this hope is not merely wistful longing and sighing for what we have not; it is a strong and confident taking refuge in God and holding fast in Him. And so we hear along with the horns of hope the strong sostenuto of the trumpets of patience, of endurance, of steadfastness. And our Ha! Ha! to that means this: "To strain towards that which is hidden as toward that which is to come, and to bear manfully the pressure of the present." (Althaus)

And we do not hope gropingly or blindly; with the trumpet of patience and with the horn of hope there come also the rolling tones of the horns of revelation. We are given eyes of the heart enlightened to know what is the hope of our calling, what are the riches of the glory of the inheritance which God has provided for us. And thus the fanfare and the flourishes of the trumpets of eternity are ringing in our ears, even here and now: "Blessed are the poor in spirit, for theirs *is* the kingdom of heaven." Oh, snuff the air of that eternal dawn, and stamp that conquered ground, that earth where God's will shall be perfectly done as it is done in heaven! Oh, snuff that air, and stamp that ground, and greet these horns with a brave Ha! Ha! "The God of hope fill you with all joy in believing."

These are the makings of your ministry. Perhaps you have decided to work like a horse in your ministry. Do so by all means. But do not work like a drudging nag under the lash, or a weary bag of bones under the yoke. We are not under the yoke in our ministry. The necessity which is laid upon us is not that of the yoke and the lash but that of the irresistible call of God's own trumpet. This is the will of God in Christ Jesus concerning your ministry.

II. *The Blasts of Satan: "Pray Without Ceasing."*

In the same breath with his command to rejoice, St. Paul bids us pray without ceasing, and he has good reason to do so. For Satan has his trumpet too. The trumpet of Satan can really sound only retreat and defeat: "Now is the judgment of this world. Now shall the prince of this world be cast out," our Lord said as He went to the cross. And the cross is an accomplished and triumphant fact. Satan has lost his right and place as the accuser of mankind; he can no longer stand before the throne of God and accuse us and our brethren day and night. He is cast out of the judgment hall, but he still has a great fury and formidable might — and deep guile. Satan is a master of the deceptive rearguard action, and he is a very tricky trumpeter. He can make his retreat sound like a very taking and attractive thing for our poor deafened and deceivable ears, and our beguiled wits are so often fools for his trumpeting. To say Ha! Ha! to God's trumpets amid the competing blasts of Satan becomes a struggle and an agony, an act of will.

We shall not have to worry about the plain frontal attack of Satan. Nobody ever was attracted to Satan himself; nobody ever found him fascinating when he showed himself for what he is. It is only when he looks like something or somebody else that he is able to win men. And so we shall not often hear, nor need we greatly fear, the nasty, brassy, vacuous trumpet of the undisguised straight satanic attack.

Satan works more cleverly and more fearfully than that. Where God sounds His trumpets of repentance, forgiveness, and love, where He summons us to deny ourselves and to spend our lives strenuously in self-giving love, Satan puts his trumpet to his lips and calls the smooth tones of seduction to ease. He calls us to consider "the good things of life," to "take it easy, watch *yourself*." And note what Satan is doing with that trumpet call of "watch yourself!" He is setting us back to where we were before God's searching love found us. He is making us men once more, men curved in upon themselves, as Luther calls them; he is making us the involuted men turned from God and in rebellion against God. They sound like pleasant notes, these trumpets of Satan. They sound like what our Lord calls the "deceit of wealth." We preachers and teachers often think that these words of the Lord about the deceit of wealth are not a text for us because we usually have so little wealth and we deem it impossible that that little should ever deceive us. But it is Satan's delight to make a man sell his soul cheap, and a little wealth can deceive as thoroughly and as fatefully as a lot of wealth. And the trumpets of Satan can delude us into preferring a little narrow, air-conditioned shelter with all the automatic advantages here on earth to the eternal mansions with their alleluiatic air above.

Satan has other trumpets too, tootling, pleasant trumpets of distraction, procrastination, and delay; he has one that plays an easy, lilting, and seductive melody entitled "A man's gotta relax sometime." Satan convinces us with this trumpet that easy fun is better than strenuous joy, and so he makes of the war horses of God fat and broken-winded jades. Or he lulls us with the soporific sameness of the trumpets of routine and monotony. He has trumpets that speak both to the lazy and to the industrious.

But Satan's master trumpet is the teasing trumpet of discontent. Note how it sings to what we like to call the frustrated pastor: "You, a man with your gifts, with your ability, your talents, with your sweet, sweet, sweet personality — stuck away here among these people, these people who have nothing to challenge you, who have nothing to recommend them (except that fact that Christ died for them, and this the satanic trumpet does *not* say); you're too good for this place!" And so the trumpet tone goes on and convinces us in the end that we are too good for almost any place, at least any place that our church could provide for us. Aggrieved, we finally feel that we ought to be giving harp lessons to an advanced group of angels.

And where God's trumpet call to confession sounds, Satan has his trumpet too. We hear the thin and slick and slimy trumpet tones of doubt: "Yea, hath God said?" — "We believe, teach and confess, — well, yes, in a sense and up to a point. But in the full and rigorous and exclusive sense of the 16th century? Well. . . ." Or he meets that call of God

9

with the perfected harmony of the trumpets of compromise: "Why be so Lutheran that it hurts? What good can come of it?"

And over against God's trumpets of hope and patience and endurance, over against the athletic resilience of divine hope, Satan sets his trumpets (and we hear them especially at times of weariness and inner exhaustion), his trumpets with their dead and flat descending tones of melancholy and despair. He makes us wallow in the luxury of melancholy, for melancholy is always a piece of pride. We feel superior — we are so sensitive, so high strung. We wish we could be as simple and untouched as the naive and busy men around about us who do their work untroubled by the complexity of our more subtle ego.

Or Satan can catch us with the monody of despair:

> Even such is time that takes in trust
> Our youth, our joys, our all we have
> And pays us but with earth and dust;
> Who in the dark and silent grave,
> When we have wandered all our ways,
> Shuts up the story of our days.

And Satan can make us quite forget the triumphant last two lines:

> But from this earth, this grave, this dust,
> My God shall raise me up, I trust.

Macbeth found that when he had the most need of blessing, the Amen stuck in his throat; and we shall find that when we have most need of hope our Ha! Ha! will stick in our throats. And so we know why St. Paul bids us pray *without ceasing,* lest the satanic trumpets take us unawares. Pray continually for the given gift, for the present benison of the trumpet call of God. Show us wondrous things out of Thy Word! O Father, let me see Thy Father's face! Oh, set the horn once more to Thy tremendous lips and blow, triumphant Trumpeter. Beat down, blast out, this nether music of temptation and despair. Set all Thine everlasting hills a-rolling with the reverberant and brazen glory of Thy victorious cry: "Jesus is Lord, Jesus is Lord, to the glory of God the Father!"

III. *"In All Things Give Thanks."*

And before we have done with our prayer, and beyond what we ask, and clearer than we could conceive, His trumpet sounds once more. Or rather, we know to our shame and to our joy that His trumpets have not failed; *we* have failed. That blast of God was ringing round us all the while. And so we breathe again, we repentant sinners, we repentant ministers, and the air we breathe is charged with the joy of God and all His angels, their joy at one sinner who repents. And the broken-down and sway-backed, jaded nag of our forgetful, sorry, fretful self becomes again the war horse of God, who snuffs the air and stamps the ground and cries Ha! Ha! among the trumpets!

We learn to make our requests known to God with thanksgiving; we learn to give thanks *in all things*. Our lives become a gamut of gratitude, no less. Not only in word — the whole tone and tenor and cadence of our life is gratitude, a resolute confession to the fact that God's trumpets are there and are mighty trumpets, mightier than all else, and that we are there to hear them.

These are the terms you serve on; these are the syllables that spell your ministry: "Rejoice — pray — give thanks." These will free you from the accent on yourself; you will not be tempted to bind others to yourself, to your ideas, to your personality; you will bind them to the God of your joy, the God whose trumpet call rings in your ears. You will be freed from yourself for others, for your flock, for your brethren. You will be full and rich in resources of comfort and strength; you will be there to strengthen the feeble knees

11

and sustain the slackened hands of affliction. You will become an echoing wall for the strong and comforting Gospel of God.

You mothers and fathers and all who have saved and scrimped and sacrificed to make this day possible for these candidates for the holy ministry: Be glad of it, rejoice in it not only for the gratitude which comes to you this day from them and which will be a light in your life in all the years to come, but be glad because you have given your sons to glory; you have matched their life with music. And you too, in your place and in your way, have spoken a brave and unforgotten Ha! Ha! to the great trumpets of God. Amen.

2

VISION FOR COMBAT

Finally, my brethren, be strong in the Lord and in the power of His might. Put on the whole armor of God that ye may be able to stand against the wiles of the devil.

For we wrestle not against flesh and blood, but against principalities, against powers, against the rulers of the darkness of this world, against spiritual wickedness in high places. Wherefore take unto you the whole armor of God that ye may be able to withstand in the evil day, and having done all, to stand.

EPHESIANS 6:10-13

The official title of this sermon is "Vision for Combat." It could also be entitled "Second Thoughts on the Way Home from the Devil's Funeral." For that is what is wrong with us in our generation. We have all been to the devil's funeral, and we have stayed for the coffee served by his grieving relatives for those who came from a distance. We have buried the devil; not officially, of course. A lot of brilliant books are still being written about him. But for how many of us is he still the living reality that he was for Martin Luther, so that the request for defense against him creeps quite naturally into our morning and evening prayers, as it did into Martin Luther's morning and evening prayers?

We are walking home from the devil's funeral, but somehow this walk home is an uneasy business. We begin to ask ourselves: Who *was* it that was in that coffin? It was never opened. And why did the devil's kinfolk take his death with such calm? The ancient and honorable family of the Diaboli are reserved people, but they are not given to taking defeat kindly. They usually howl and gnash their teeth. And what is that shadow behind the tree?

On our way home St. Paul is a good man to meet. He did not attend the devil's funeral. He was too realistic for that. He knows that the devil is not dead. He knows it much better than we do. He knows that Satan is very much alive, and he knows that the devil is on the prowl, and St. Paul is not ignorant of his devices. St. Paul knows that battle is inevitable, and he knows, too, what it is like. He knows (1) that it is tricky, (2) that it is lonely, and (3) that it can be won.

It is tricky. "Stand against the wiles of the devil!" Satan is a lot more sophisticated than we are. He has lived longer, and he has observed the human race very closely, with all the intensity of hatred, for all these centuries. And so the one certain thing about his *modus operandi* is that he will not use the one you have last been warned about. You can feed all his past operations into a computer, but it cannot classify his *modus operandi,* and it cannot forecast it. He is master of variety — "We are legion." And so whenever we speak of the devil, we have to speak generally, we have to speak in "e. g.'s." One thing is sure: the attack will be in unlikely ways and in unlikely places. St. Paul himself sees the satanic attack in operation not so much in the world as in the church itself. He knows that Satan likes the stratagem of religiosity. When brisk new theological movements developed in the church, St. Paul said: "God will crush Satan under your feet shortly." The new "Christ" men at Corinth — St. Paul says they are emissaries of the devil.

14

He described a man intoxicated on the new theology as both drunk and caught in a net, a blundering drunk who got himself wrapped up in the devil's fishnet. The only salvation for him is to get sober and get out of that net.

Another stratagem Satan was famous for, one that you can depend on, is the stratagem of frustration. Whenever you see a problem everyone recognizes, an evil everybody knows, one everybody is working on and nobody seems to be able to find a cure for, there Satan is at work. You might call this the "Seven Maids and the Seven Mops" situation:

> "If seven maids with seven mops
> Should sweep for half a year,
> Do you suppose," the Walrus said,
> "That they could get it clear?"
> "I doubt it," said the Carpenter,
> And shed a bitter tear.

The whole church every so often is in the carpenter's plight, inclined to shed his bitter tears over these problems of frustration. The whole church can go baying down the wrong trail on a wrong scent, concentrating on a problem that does not particularly need solving to begin with. We could speak of "transsubjective forces" at work in denominations and churches in all Christendom, but we might as well give the dog a name and call it Satan because that is what it is.

Another favorite stratagem of Satan is the stratagem of weariness and (closely connected with it) self-pity. Satan has the high art of making us feel noble in our vices. There never yet was a slob that did not somehow feel superior to some other slob. I have met a lot of them, and I have never known one yet that did not fit that pattern. That is a satanic device. Take one that is close to us. You are tired. Satan can make us feel awfully noble about our weariness, our tiredness. We have really been slugging it out, but the question we have to ask in this tricky battle is: Am I tired from work, or am I tired because I don't want to work anymore? There is quite a difference. When you're young you wonder why sloth was included among the seven deadly sins. Acedia is for us, then, a remote and untried sin. As you get older, not too much older, you begin to know; you begin to know how satanic the temptation of melancholy and resignation really is, how like being trapped in a cave with cobwebs of inertia across your eyes and across your mouth. You feel mysterious, loathsome bat wings brushing you; they are the rationalizations that you do not believe even while you are making them, that you loathe even while you frame them.

Another satanic stratagem is that of perverted priorities. There is always something we have to do *first*. It is not quite so important, but it is more pressing. We all know this one — but do we always recognize it as satanic?

The agony of freedom is another one of Satan's stratagems. We grow tired of liberty; we cannot bear the freedom with which Christ has set us free. We long for a tyrannous bishop to tell exactly what to do. We long for a martinet of an abbot to spell it out: "Thus far and no farther!" We should like to believe what the church believes and let the church worry about it. That would put an end to all exegesis and systematics and a lot of other things besides.

The worst satanic stratagem is that his attacks are so autobiographical. They are so personal. We look into the face of our adversary, and we recognize our own features. He always attacks us with weapons that we have furnished. Satan's suggestions are always in the last analysis *my* suggestions. There has been a prize contest, and we have all written little essays for Satan, e. g., "I Like Sinning Because." Our little 25-word essays are those he uses against us.

It is a tricky battle; it is not against flesh and blood. We deal with the superhuman, with the faceless, the contourless, the formless, the nonidentifiable power. All the terror of vagueness, all the terror of the nonmeasurable, the non-calculable, the nonpalpable — that is in this battle. We deal with rulers of the darkness of this world. We are in the land of ambiguities; we can identify our adversary only by his grunts and scufflings, only by the loathsome smell of his sweat. We are in the land of senseless panic, of self-generated and self-perpetuating fear, of senseless cowardice and equally senseless self-confidence.

This is spiritual wickedness in high places, "in the heavenly places," Paul says. With a heart a man believes, and in the heart the battle is fought. Just where we meet the blessing of the elective love of God, there we meet this Satan. Just where we meet the enthroning love of God (He has made us sit in the high places with Christ), there we meet the satanic power. Both are overarching, transcendent powers, intruding into our lives at every point.

It is a tricky battle, and it is a lonely one. Paul says, "We *wrestle*," that is, man to man; that is, one man alone — only two can play. We are alone, but the fearful thing about this match is that the other side is not alone. We wrestle with a collusive, a concatenated, a concerted, a concentrated power of darkness. All are against us, principalities, powers, and rulers. And there is no collective security here. This we have to do alone.

> You were born alone;
> You'll die alone.
> So learn a lesson, little one,
> All things difficult are done
> Alone, alone, alone.

It is true, no man is an island, and God has bound us each to each. We hear one another's battle cries and are heartened by one another's triumphs and warned by one another's failures. But if no man is an island, no man is an orchestra either. He has to play his part if the orchestra is to play. And if that part is only three little toots at the end of the Fourth Movement, he has to be there for those three little toots.

It is a fearful battle, and it is a lonely one; but it can be won. That is hard for us to believe. We are alone, we are open-eyed, we have shed the delusion of the devil's funeral. We are terrified, we are desperate, we know where we stand, we know the enemy, we know our own weakness. But self-pity and self-analysis is not going to help us here anymore. And yet Paul says, "Be strong!" Our first reaction is, "Who? Me? Me? With my knees knocking?"

But Paul says, "Be strong *in the Lord*," be *strengthened* in the Lord; find your strength in the Lord and in the power of His might. This battle can be won because it *has* been won by our Lord and Savior Jesus Christ, who enclosed us all in His almighty love. Take on the armor of God; that panoply is His pure gift to us. Take it, receive it, and wear it. Wear it as your dress, your daily dress, and keep on wearing it. It was David Thoreau who said that it takes about three years before a man's pants start fitting him, and something of this holds of this, the armor of God. It grows on us; it fits itself to us; it accommodates itself to us by daily use. Let us wear that armor of God. Let us not turn to self-analysis. Let us write the words that Luther wrote on the table before him in those dreadful moments of solitary despair: *Baptizatus sum!* "I have been baptized!" That is a present perfect. When God took hold of my life and made me His own, He did it for keeps. He clothed me in that armor. "This is My body, this is My blood," our Lord has said, for keeps. These are weapons.

And His words are weapons too. "Behold I put My words in thy mouth; I have made thee this day a defenced city and an iron pillar and a brazen wall." With this armor we can withstand, and we can stand. We need not crawl, and we dare not dance. The time for dancing in the streets is not yet. Now is the time to withstand and stand. Once we think we can start dancing, it is all over. There is no instant victory here. Nothing quick and nothing easy; we cannot just add water and serve. This is blood and sweat and tears. And it goes on as long as this world stands. But we shall learn who our enemy is, and that one little word can stop him. We shall learn who our Lord is, we shall learn what our armor is. Our "Get thee gone, Satan!" may be weak and squeaky at first, but we shall learn to speak it with increasing strength. We speak it and — strange! — in the midst of tumult and shouting and conflict the peace of God which passeth all understanding is ours even there, just there. Amen.

3

FEAR BORN OF FORGIVENESS

(Advent)

But there is forgiveness with Thee that Thou mayest be feared.
PSALM 130:4

The psalmist has cried to God out of the depths, out of the depths which the sin of man has dug. He has cried to God, before whom no man can stand: "If Thou, Lord, shouldest mark iniquities, O Lord, who shall stand?" He has cried to God, before whose majesty every mouth is stopped and at whose righteous tribunal all the world must plead guilty. But He has found God to be the Lord, the God of Israel, the Savior, the covenant God, the God of causelessly elective love, the God who answered Moses' plea, "Show me Thy glory," show me Thy quintessential Godhead, with the words: "I will make all My goodness to pass before thee, and I will proclaim the name of the Lord before thee, and I will be gracious, and I will show mercy." He had found Him to be the Lord with whom is mercy and plenteous redemption. And he can from his own encounter with this God proclaim to his brethren: "He shall redeem Israel, the people of God, from all their iniquities."

And it is here, just at this point, in this confrontation with the God of mercy and of plenteous redemption, that holy fear is born. "There is forgiveness with Thee that Thou mayest be feared." The high majesty of God has spoken this word of forgiveness; the great King has forgiven His slave that immeasurable and insurmountable debt. "In that God forgives sin He shows Himself mightier than sin; and since He alone has power to overcome sin by His forgiveness, He is to be feared as the forgiving God, too, yes, just as the forgiving God." (A. Weiser)

In the forgiving Word of God the incomprehensible greatness of God, the intolerable glory of His Godhead, the glory of His grace, has appeared, has appeared to eyes that cannot comprehend it even as they gaze upon it. It has been manifested to hearts that stand in trembling awe of it even as they believe it. This grace of which the psalmist sings is no cheap, easy grace, no easy commodity which complacency can casually appropriate. We can be sure of it, surer of it than of ourselves, than of our righteousness or our sins or our life or our death. But we cannot be complacent about it. Our souls still wait for the Lord, more than the watchmen that wait for the morning. They know that morning will come; they are sure that it will come, and yet they wait for it, and they hail its first graying as a new and wondrous thing. So we wait for the Lord and know that He is Lord and will forgive. But forgiveness remains the perpetual miracle still. God as Forgiver is the Object of our fear. Luther spells it out negatively. "O God," he says, "if all did not depend upon Thy mercy, if we could remove sin by our power, no one would fear Thee, and the whole world would in its pride despise Thee." Or again, with remorseless logic, he says: "I lay this syllogism upon your heart: Where there is no forgiveness, there is no God. Likewise, where God is not,

there is no forgiveness. Likewise, where there is no forgiveness, there is no fear of God. There idolatry and righteousness of works abide."

"There is forgiveness with Thee that Thou mayest be
feared." These words might well serve as a caption over
all the words and works of John the Baptist, that great Advent preacher. For this holy fear of which the psalmist speaks
is in all that he says and does. We behold him in Scripture,
come in the spirit and power of Elijah, being very jealous
for the Lord God, never letting us forget how great and fearful this one God is, this God who will not give His glory to
another, never letting us forget how wide and deep the gulf
is across which He in infinite condescension offers Himself
for communion to us. He never lets us forget how deep the
depths are from which the voice of our supplication must
arise.

John proclaims the nearness of the reign of God, and the
coming of that reign, the coming in of the kingdom of God,
is pure, unalloyed, and perfect grace. But that grace is God's
great "Nevertheless," the never-to-be-expected "Nevertheless" to the divine wrath, that wrath which impends in ex-
ceptionless rigor on man as man, on man who is by birth
and being a generation of vipers. And that grace of God has
with it always, as the cast shadow of its brightness, God's
fearful judgment on grace rejected and on grace misused.
Every tree which brings not forth good fruit is hewn down
and cast into the fire.

The Mightier One whom John heralds comes with the
Baptism of spirit, with the creative breath of God that makes
the desert bloom and makes dead bones rise. But He comes
also with the fire of God's inexorable judgment. He brings
home the winnowed grain into His barn, but He burns the
chaff with unquenchable fire. "Behold the Lamb of God

that taketh away the sins of the world!" he cries. That is God's answer, God's triumphant answer to the sin of rebellious man, God's mighty and victorious reachdown into the depths from which we must cry. But it is a costly answer, and it is the only answer. For this Lamb is God's eternal Son, who was first, before John. And to reject this answer of God is to come, more, it is to remain, under the wrath of God. This Lamb is the Mightier One, mightier far than John, mightier than the greatest of woman-born, so great, so tremendous in His servile majesty that even John could not ultimately serve Him. John could not comprehend Him, as his question from prison shows, "Art Thou He?" Even John could do only one thing: John could only believe on Him.

It is not accidental that we hear that John taught his disciples to pray. Prayer is born of fear and faith. Faith knows that God has loved me with an everlasting love; faith is certain: "God has chosen me"; faith knows: "God has laid His hand upon me and called me His." But that certainly shows itself constantly, practically, in prayer. Faith knows that the brother standing beside me is the object of God's elective love, that God has loved him with an everlasting love. But that certainty works itself out in constant intercession. An Advent life is a life of prayer in holy fear and a life of intercession.

We who give ear to the voice of John, we who follow the pointing finger of John, that great Advent preacher, can never take Christ for granted, can never grow casual about Him and His mercy. Nor can we who have heard the Baptist's Advent cry ever think of repentance as a placid, pious exercise, a sort of routine religious daily dozen. It is the death of the old man and the creation of the new man as God's own.

Nor will we ever again think of Baptism as the subject

23

for a cozy family festival, where parents beam and aunts coo and uncles make funny faces. It is a Baptism of repentance, unto repentance, for the forgiveness of sins. It is God's rescue of the lost and desperate, "that He may be feared."

If we follow the finger of John, we cannot make of Advent and Christmas a sort of ecclesiastical bacchanalia. We welcome our Lord "in strains of holy joy." This is no cheap grace that John the Baptist proclaims either, something that we can complacently accept as a matter of fact, something that our pride can reject in order to pick up later, something that our eloquence can mouth; it is the costly, the pure, the true grace of God, "that He may be feared."

And if we let this Advent witness, this witness to the light, John the Baptist, loom large before our eyes, we shall never be able to think of the witnessing church as a going concern, as a self-originating and self-perpetuating body. Our witnessing, our missionary work, will be done in awe and fear. "He must increase, I must decrease." And our life as a church will be lived throughout in the awesome conviction, the Advent conviction, that upon us the ends of the world have come, that in us and through us God is writing His last great chapter of grace and judgment with Spirit and with fire. And the words of the psalmist will live in our hearts and on our lips with a new intensity: "There is forgiveness with Thee that Thou mayest be feared." Amen.

4

HE SHALL BE GREAT

(Advent)

He shall be great in the sight of the Lord. — LUKE 1:15

These are, of course, the words of the angel Gabriel concerning John the Baptist. John the Baptist is the only man in the New Testament who is called great in a laudatory sense, except, of course, the Man Jesus Christ, our Lord and Savior. And yet he of all men is totally unconcerned about any greatness of his own; for his greatness is an Advent greatness, the greatness of a man for whom the great question in history is no longer, What is coming? What will become of me? but, Who is coming? It is a *coram Domino* greatness, a greatness whose sole concern is the Coming One, the Mightier One, the Savior and the Judge. It is as if he had laid his life in the hands of his coming Lord, almost blithely, with an almost debonair air, and said: "Lord, have a care of my life; Lord, have a care of my greatness, if any. I haven't time for it myself; I'm going to be much too busy." And by that act John became great, great with an Advent greatness, with the only greatness that has any place or validity among men who are concerned about the Deliverer and Savior and Judge who is coming, the only greatness possible in the church, whose year begins with the season of Advent, whose cry, therefore, is *Maran-atha!* "Our Lord, come!"

What does it look like, this greatness of John the Baptist, this Advent greatness? It is marked, first of all, by a great and free independence. By throwing himself wholly upon God and upon His greater Coming One, and by depending completely upon Him, John made himself free of everyone else and of everything else. He was free from the passion for conformity to patterns. He broke them all. He broke the Judaic pattern. He called his people out into the wilderness; he called men away from the settled sanctities of the temple and the synagogs, from all their hallowed habituations, and called them into the desert to confront there the bare majesty of the God whom Israel knew before Israel had settled sanctities, before there was a Holy Land, a Holy City, a holy temple, and a cultus. He cut across that pattern with a vengeance. He paid little heed to the Herodian pattern, and it was a pattern to be feared. Its iron outlines ultimately cut off John's head. But John did not become the super-serviceable knave in soft raiment. He remained John the Baptist. A cobweb in the October air could not have influenced him and shaped him less than did this iron pattern. The Pharisaic and the Sadducean patterns did not concern him either, although Pharisee and Sadducee paid him the compliment of coming to his Baptism and were content to bask for a while in him as the burning and shining light. And that too despite the fact that he, like Jesus, had more in common with the Pharisees — Scriptures, awe for the will of God, the Messianic hope, the resurrection of the dead — he had more in common with the Pharisees than with any other group under the sun. He declined also to fit himself into the popular Messianic pattern and to do the people's will although that was a real possibility. According to Josephus, the realistic Herod feared him and hated him for that reason also.

John fitted into nobody's pattern and was concerned about nobody's pattern. Neither the somebodies nor the nobodies ever knew quite what to make of him. We are a gregarious pack, and so we cannot ever be quite comfortable in the presence of the verdict "great," which our Lord pronounces upon John. We with our awed respect for patterns, our passion for belonging, our avidity for acceptance, our yearning for the security of a certified mediocrity, our fear of renouncing the majority. It's nice to be normal, it's nice to be accepted, it's nice to belong, scholastically, sociologically, civically, theologically, ecumenically, and, bless the mark, even philosophically.

With independence comes that quality which we find hard to give a single name to. The Bible calls it *parrhesia,* boldness, confidence, the courage for antagonism, if you will. John breasted the terrifying current of public opinion by admitting to his Baptism the harlot, the Gentile soldier, and the parish publican. He called Pharisee and Sadducee a generation of vipers and pulled the rug of their genealogy out from under their feet. He told Herod, "It is not right for thee to have her." And he bade all Israel, without exception, all the pietists of penance, all the hierarchy, everybody, to put themselves on a level with the dirty Gentile and be washed with his Baptism of repentence unto the remission of sin. Does this quite square with our idea of the good, solid church in a good, solid neighborhood, with a nice sign out in front, the church which pays its debts, including the debt of lip service to a pattern, and is known and loved by all?

It is a greatness, furthermore, of concentration. Greatness eliminates ruthlessly. It is a greatness obsessed with a sense of eschatological urgency that knows, like St. Paul, that the time has been contracted. "How much time is there?" this greatness asks. John was a Nazirite with absolute devotion. And he was a monomaniac. He was known by one name only, the Baptist. And his one self-designation is "Voice." The disciples of John? One may doubt whether they had a very well-rounded program. How well-rounded can you be in this contraction aeon? How much room is there for roundness? How much need does God have for roundness? Perhaps He can use a few monomaniacs, with jagged edges. How much time is there, let us ask ourselves, for gewgaws, for gimcracks, for all manner of tiddlywinks? We are in God's last chapter. We are walking between contracting walls of time, and anybody who bears a pack of peripheries is walking down that corridor at his peril. We are in God's last chapter, and nobody knows how close the last sentence (and a *sentence* it will be) of that chapter is. How much room is there on that page for irrelevant footnotes?

And last, this greatness of John is a greatness of subordination. This is the greatest of all. "I am not Elijah, I am not the prophet, I am not the Christ; I take no title, not even Elijah, unless my Lord wants to give it to me. I am but a Voice crying in the wilderness. I am exhausted in my function of crying: 'Repent ye, be baptized, look to the Greater One.' He must increase; I must decrease. This is my joy, and this my joy is full." John had no bigness to get in the way of his greatness, and therefore he had no jealousy to darken the bright joy of his subordinate greatness. We find this greatness reflected in St. Paul: "What then? So Christ be preached, I do rejoice, and I will rejoice."

John the Baptist paid the price for this kind of greatness, for this greatness of independence, of confidence, of concentration, of absolute subordination. Men twiddled theological thumbs at him and did not make up their minds about him. They swathed him in the whipped cream of their indecision. Is his Baptism from heaven? We do not know. They treated him as one of a number of theological lights — stimulating, provocative. They rejoiced for a season in this burning lamp. And ultimately their verdict was: "He hath a devil." In modern parlance: "He's psychopathic. He's compensating for something. He's narrow; he's one-sided." No answer of John the Baptist to these critiques is recorded; but the whole record of his life cries out, "Who cares? Who cares?"

So we are funny-looking figures too, we who inherit John the Baptist's mouth, finger, and voice, as Luther put it. We are odd, misplaced-looking fellows, a curious sort of gentry, as we catch sight of our reflection in the shop windows of the world. Well, who cares? Who cares? So nobody who is anybody thinks we are somebody. Who cares? — There was somebody who cared, and somebody who cares, if we will enter upon the heritage of John the Baptist, if we will take up John's finger, John's mouth, and John's voice and cry, "Repent!" and point to Christ and call Him Lord. The Coming One, the Mightier One, cares. The Son of God, who loved us and gave Himself for us, the Lamb of God that takes away the sins of the world, He cares. John renounced all bigness, and he became great in the sight of the Lord. Jesus cared. Jesus called him the greatest of woman-born, called him a prophet, and more than a prophet, called him the messenger foretold by Malachi to prepare the way of the Lord, called him the returning Elijah, asserted that his Baptism was from heaven, and said that his way was the way of righteousness. He cared. And if we will enter upon the heritage of John the Baptist, we shall know that He cares for us. We shall one day hear from His lips: "Well done, thou good and faithful servant! Enter into the joy of thy Lord."

This peculiar greatness, this unsought and unseeking greatness, this unrecognized greatness, is therefore not a misfortune, not a "cross" which the church must assume with a sigh, not something to be taken up somehow, anyhow; it is a blessing and a delight, and it is that even here, even now. It is the blessedness of the soul that is like a weaned child. "Lord, my heart is not haughty . . . neither do I exercise myself in great matters. . . . Surely, I have behaved and quieted myself as a child that is weaned of his mother. My soul is even as a weaned child" (Ps. 131). Our delight is to be with God, not because He can supply us with something, with greatness, for instance, but because He is our God and because He loves us.

This was not the man, John, of course, that achieved this greatness. It was the man whom God sent; it was he who was filled with the Holy Ghost from his mother's womb, even as we are filled with the Holy Ghost from our Baptism on. That was the enabling power of his greatness. And so, as we speak and sing of the Holy Spirit, we pay a real tribute to the real greatness, the Advent greatness of John the Baptist. Amen.

5

"IF WE WALK IN THE LIGHT"

(Epiphany)

This, then, is the message which we have heard of Him and declare unto you, that God is Light and in Him is no darkness at all. If we say that we have fellowship with Him and walk in darkness, we lie and do not the truth. But if we walk in the light, as He is in the light, we have fellowship one with another, and the blood of Jesus Christ, His Son, cleanseth us from all sin. If we say that we have no sin, we deceive ourselves, and the truth is not in us. If we confess our sins, He is faithful and just to forgive us our sins and to cleanse us from all unrighteousness. If we say that we have not sinned, we make Him a liar, and His Word is not in us. — 1 JOHN 1:5-10

We all know what Epiphany means: "Thy Light is come, and the Glory of the Lord is risen upon thee," in the words of Isaiah, or "God is Light, and in Him is no darkness at all," according to St. John. Where we stand has become holy ground: "Put off thy shoes from off thy feet!"

God looms so large, so bright, in the beauty of His holiness. We grow so small, so ugly; we can't endure the light, and yet we don't want darkness either. However, we know a thing or two; we put up parasols to stand between the full light and us, to keep us in a sort of twilight zone, a spot of shade between light and darkness, and take our Epiphany in diffusion and dodge the *"is no darkness at all."*

First Parasol

"If we say that we have fellowship with Him and walk in darkness."

This, like most satanic tricks, is not as hard as it looks, and a really clever Christian can do it a hundred times in a day. You don't have to come out and say anything about what you're doing — in fact, the best part of the trick is not even to think about your stroll in the darkness. You sing Hallelujah, Hosanna, and Amen in four parts, *a cappella,* and just act as if darkness weren't darkness. Well, perhaps not pure light either, just a deepish shade of gray. You study the configuration of a man's ears during a sermon — nothing so very dark about that, except of course that God put that preacher with that sermon there for you, and that the tension of the bent bow of His Word is in that sermon too. I walk in darkness when I decide that for all practical purposes I am more important than God and His Word.

St. John, the apostle of love, even he, just he, for there is nothing so stringent as love, nothing so inexorable, strips off the silk of this parasol for us and snaps the ribs and breaks the handle over his knee and leaves us with a mess about our feet; but we are in the light again: "We lie and do not the truth." — We lie as surely as if we had put it into so many words, for we do not the truth; for this truth is Epiphany, this truth is light, this truth is life and must be lived. St. John brought back no theory from his communion with Jesus, no set of propositions, no ideas; he brought a message, intended for us, confronting us, a word that takes us captive, restores and recreates us. God does not lecture to us in the apostolic Word; He confronts us in the glory of His grace, a grace that we dare not receive in vain.

Second Parasol

There is another parasol, and St. John deals with that one too: *"If we say that we have no sin."* Not one of us will say it outright, but we believe it enough to act on it nevertheless. We act as if sin were a dead issue in our lives, as if we had no sin that doth easily beset us, that needs to be resisted to the blood; as if the roaring lion who walketh about, seeking whom he may devour, were not allowed to roam our streets; as if the evil day were not in my calendar and the whole armor of God could rust in my closet; as if some good thing dwelt in my flesh after all; as if I could skate on thin ice in the snug assurance that those unfathomable and icy waters are there to drown others and not me. Where is the fear and trembling in our lives that makes our hold on God, who works in us both to will and to do, the ceaseless hold of desperation?

This parasol goes to the rubbish heap too. *"We deceive ourselves"* — the fault is ours, not God's, in whom is no darkness at all — *"and the truth is not in us."* We thrust it from us, this truth, slide out from under it, *the* truth, the only truth that can make us free, the light, the eternal light without which no man can live. We want a little shade; we did not bargain for this darkness.

Third Parasol

"If we say that we have not sinned."

Need we pursue our clever little parasol maker further? Surely we confess our sins, surely we are Christians enough for that. But this is St. John the apostle speaking, and he speaks in the first person plural. We had better face it and see our last parasol go smash like the rest. Oh, yes, we confess that we have sinned — by chapter certainly and by paragraph perhaps; but what about the sentence and the word? The specific sin, the one just past, especially the little one just past, do I confess that too?

"If we say that we have not sinned, we make Him a liar, and His Word is not in us." His Son taught us the Lord's Prayer, including the Fifth Petition, and we want to pray it with revisions. His word is: "There is none that is righteous, no, not one." His word is: "The Son of Man came to seek and to save that which was lost." . . . And we would deny it, refuse it. — And there is no other word but His — "to whom, Lord, shall we go?"

There goes our last parasol. We stand before the brightness of the glory of God alone and bare. Turn! Repent! Turn to the light! How hard it is! How Mr. Ego clutches and tugs to hold us back. But he is gone now, and we are free of him, alone with God — and lo! what we have dreaded is not dreadful at all. That voice of love, whose words stripped us bare, clothes us in garments whiter than the snow, bright with the imparted holiness of God's creative light: we have come into a field of energy, of life — we walk in light even as He is in the light.

"If we confess our sins, He is faithful and just to forgive us our sins and to cleanse us from all unrighteousness." — He is faithful, He is just, even when we are faithless and when we sin. He holds to His Word that He spoke to us in His Son, the Word of grace and truth; He keeps the covenant that He has sealed with the blood of His own, His only-begotten Son. *"The blood of Jesus Christ, His Son, cleanseth us from all sin."* The ever new, the ever incredible miracle of the

forgiveness of sins by God's grace, for Christ's sake, shines forth in glad Epiphany. All that sundered us from God, all that sundered us from one another, is gone, is dealt with. It is as if it never had been. We have fellowship one with another, we are a church once more, and we are glad again with an exceeding great joy. Amen.

6

THE DISCIPLES' CONFESSION

(Lent)

Then Jesus said to them, "You will all fall away because of Me this night; for it is written, 'I will strike the Shepherd, and the sheep of the flock will be scattered.'" — MATTHEW 26:31

The story of the Passion of our Lord has been recorded for us by His disciples. And not the least remarkable feature of that remarkable record is the fact that it is the record, unblinking, and unvarnished, of the disciples' failure. That failure is sharply defined by the record. The disciples were not overtaken unawares by the cross; they were not surprised by the cross; they were simply overwhelmed by it.

The disciples failed in spite of the fact that Jesus had predicted just this event as the end, and not only the end but as the goal of His mission on earth. Jesus had foretold His death no less than three times before it took place: (1) at Caesarea Philippi, after the disciples had confessed Him as the Christ, the Son of the living God; (2) in Galilee, after the transfiguration, and (3) as He turned His face for the last time toward Jerusalem. At the time of the last Passover in Jerusalem Jesus could refer to His impending death as something familiar to His disciples: "You know that after two days the Passover is coming, and the Son of Man will be delivered up to be crucified." The disciples' failure was not failure in the face of a completely unexpected event but in the face of a predicted event.

Moreover, Jesus had not merely predicted His coming death; He had also given His disciples a profound insight into the meaning of that death. The predictions themselves had been interpretations of the event. The first prediction follows hard upon Peter's confession to Jesus as the Christ, the Son of the living God. Jesus was going to His death as the Christ, and this was no accident, no frustration of His mission, but the fulfillment of it; He went this way to Jerusalem to rejection, suffering, and death under the must of his Father's will. And therefore Jesus made it plain that He willed His death with His whole heart. When Peter objected and saw in the cross something that could not and dared not happen to Jesus, something that God simply could not permit, Jesus made absolutely no concession to Peter's thinking. He branded Peter's suggestion as satanic and trampled it underfoot. He marked Peter's will and intent as sinfully centered in man and not intent upon the things of God. And He made His cross the pattern of the whole life of the disciple: "If any man would come after Me, let him deny himself and take up his cross and follow Me."

The second prediction came after the transfiguration, after that vision of Jesus in glory which showed them Jesus, the Representative and Pioneer of the new mankind, at the goal of God's ways with mankind, transfigured, partaking of the divine glory in unabridged and unimpeded sonship. In keeping with this the prediction was given in terms of broadest universality. The way for man goes through suffering and death to glory. The Son of man is destined to be delivered up into the hands of men who shall slay Him. This time the disciples did not object; Jesus had brought them thus far. But neither could they make Jesus' will to the cross their own. They submitted to the cross, but reluctantly. "They were greatly distressed."

The third prediction, made as Jesus was about to go to Jerusalem, was the most specific and detailed of all. The Son of Man will be delivered up, and again the leaders of Israel are the instruments of Israel's rejection of the Messiah. Death is to be in full legal form, and the rejection will be complete. Here for the first time we hear of the fact that Jesus will be delivered up to the Gentiles and will die upon the cross. The rejection of the Messiah will be complete; Israel will degrade its Messiah in His death. No direct reaction of the disciples to this prediction is recorded, but the narrative which follows — the request of the sons of Zebedee for places of honor and the ensuing quarrel between them and the remaining disciples — shows that they still tended to overleap the cross and reach for the life and glory beyond it.

Not that they were wrong in seeking greatness and glory beyond the cross. Jesus Himself looked beyond the cross. Each of Jesus' predictions of his Passion had its close and climax in the foretelling of His resurrection. The same divine will that led Him into death was to lead Him farther still — to life and glory. His death was to be no frustration of his mission but a decisive part in the accomplishment of his mission. It was to be not end but transition, not defeat but victory.

But Jesus had interpreted the meaning of His death for His disciples even more fully and explicitly than this. He interpreted His death as the culmination of a life of ministry, as the giving of His life as a ransom for many (Matt. 20:28). He thereby marked His life and death and resurrection as

38

the continuation and the consummation of the Old Testament revelation of God as the God who ministers to men. He marked that ministry as a total ministry: full, voluntary, obedient self-devotion. He marked His dying as a ministry to doomed men, for the word "ransom" pronounces a verdict upon the life of man as a lost and forfeited life. He also marked His whole ministry as an expression of the unsearchable love of God, as God's gracious "nevertheless" over against the lost and doomed life of mankind. He opened up to them the full horror of His dying, the horror of a death under the wrath of the righteous God. He marked His death as a penal death, suffered for the revolt and disobedience of men.

On the night in which He was betrayed Jesus again interpreted His death for His disciples when He called His shed blood "my blood of the *covenant,* which is poured out for many for the forgiveness of sin." In describing His death in terms of the covenant Jesus was interpreting His death as the gracious will of God for men, that gracious will which had made Israel His peculiar people, which had established a covenant with David and promised the Messiah, which had shown itself in the gracious ministry of the Servant of the Lord who was to bring back Israel to the Lord and was to be a Light to all the nations. He marked His death as the fulfillment of the promise given through the prophet Jeremiah, the promise of a new covenant in which God would forgive the iniquity of His people and remember their sins no more. He marked His death as God's will for men, God's grace to men, God's deed for men, God's gift to men.

But it was not only Jesus' express prediction of His death and His explicit interpretation of His death that had prepared the disciples for the cross. This prediction and this interpretation have no markedly separate place in His words and works. The cross had been in the texture of His life from the beginning. The life of Jesus and the death of Jesus are seen by the gospels as the one seamless robe of the Christ. The disciples who were His eyewitnesses and became the ministers of His Word have left this imprint indelibly upon the record of Jesus' words and works, and they left it there because it was there to begin with. There is not a word or work of Jesus recorded anywhere in our gospels which is not in keeping with His will to take up His cross and die.

Even in the early, blithe Galilean days He had spoken to His disciples of the time when the wedding-party exuberance of their association would give way to fasting, when the Bridegroom would be "taken away" (9:15). When men challenged Him to authenticate His Messianic claim with a "sign from heaven," He promised them the sign of Jonah (12:38-41; 16:1-4), the sign connected with His death. He saw in the treatment accorded the returning Elijah, John the Baptist, in the fact that men "did to him whatever they pleased" (17:12), the pattern of His own fate and its prediction.

In the training of His disciples, when He sought to create men in His own image, He pronounced a blessing on the persecuted (5:10, 11), on men persecuted for righteousness' sake, that is, for His sake. And He set them on a narrow way and promised to bring them through a narrow gate into the Kingdom. He left them no illusions; they were following One whom the mass of men rejected (7:13, 14). When He sent out the Twelve, He sent them out as sheep among wolves, to certain and intense and universal persecution. (10:16-25)

His words have the cross in them from the beginning. His judgment on Israel and Jerusalem must be included here too; Israel is doomed because Israel has refused God's last messenger, God's Son (21:33-41). And here, as everywhere,

Jesus' works are of a piece with His words. He never forced men or overwhelmed them. His voice was the potent and persuasive calling of the mother hen, persuasive but not irresistible. He launched no massed Messianic movement. Time and again, when resistance mounted, He withdrew. His disciples came to see that motif of withdrawal even in His infancy, in the flight to Egypt (2:14, 22), and it recurs four times in Matthew (4:12; 12:15; 14:13; 15:21). He withdrew until the hour of His cross had come; then He withdrew no more.

He used His miraculous powers in complete selflessness, as the Servant ministering to others (8:17; 12:15-21). He never used the miracle to provide for Himself, to defend Himself, to advance Himself, or to escape hostility. The jibe under the cross, "He saved others; He cannot save Himself" (27-42), was true in a deeper sense than the jibers knew. He who willed the cross as His Father willed it "could" not save Himself. Jesus was as much the Suffering Servant in His earlier words and works as He was on the cross. And He was, as will become apparent, as much the Anointed King, the majestic Messiah of God, upon the cross as in the first glad ministry and in all His mighty acts.

Despite all this the disciples failed. And their failure began early, at the anointing of Jesus in the house of Simon the Leper at Bethany (26:6-13). When it was given to a woman, left nameless in Matthew, to see farther with the intuition of her believing love than the minds of the disciples for all their superior training could reach — when it was given her to recognize in Jesus the Messiah who was about to die and to anoint Him for His burial, the disciples had no understanding for her act and little sympathy for her devotion; they "troubled" the woman with their indignation and their talk of waste. The reckless splendor of this gift by one who acted so well though she knew so little was lost on men who knew so much and acted not at all.

The disciples failed. Judas, one of the Twelve, betrayed his Lord (26:14-16). The profundity of his failure and the depth of the mystery of his malice are marked by the fact that the identification of the betrayer and the institution of the Lord's Supper are set in hard juxtaposition (26:25-29); the self-seeking will of man is confronted with the self-giving will of the Messiah. But no attempt is made to plumb the mystery presented by the fact that one so favored should fall so far and so irrevocably. Indeed the objectivity and reserve of the account of Judas' fall is remarkable — there is no invective against him, no recrimination, no rhetorical underscoring of his ingratitude and guilt. The will which Jesus had shaped with His "Judge not" appears in this account, a will whose final contours the experience of the disciples in the Passion fixed. And the will which Jesus had molded with the Sixth Petition — "Lead us not into temptation" — appears in the disciples here too. The strength of Peter's devotion to his Lord might lead him to cry, "Though they all fall away because of You, I will never fall away," and "Even if I must die with You, I will not deny You" (26: 33, 35), and all the disciples might echo his resolve (there was still in them what needed to be washed away by the deep and whelming waters of their failure); yet there lived in them all also that fear and trembling which made them all "very sorrowful" when Jesus said, "One of you will betray Me", and made each one of them ask, "Is it I, Lord?" (26:20-22). Not one of them was so secure that he could not see himself in Judas' place, and the absolute objectivity of the narrative of Judas' betrayal must be set down as one of the fruits of the Passion.

Judas the betrayer is the very antipode of Judas the disciple. The mark of the disciple is the self-expending will which Jesus had implanted: "Give without pay" (10:8). The betrayal is a transaction for gain; how completely that will to give without pay had died in him, Judas reveals by his words to the chief priests, *"What will you give me* if I deliver Him to you?" (26:15). The words are an indication, too, of how empty a disciple's life becomes once Jesus no longer fills it; all that Judas has to fill that vacuum is money.

The disciples failed. The three whom Jesus took with Him when He withdrew to pray slept in Gethsemane (26:36-46). They could no longer deprecate the cross, as Peter had done when Jesus first foretold it (16:22). They hardly had the heart anymore for the great sorrow they had felt at the second announcement of the Passion (17:22, 23). The dreams of pride and place which had made them reach beyond the cross to the subsequent glory at the third announcement of the Passion (20:20-28) had evaporated now, and they were left flat and empty, overwhelmed by a melancholy lethargy. And so they simply shut out the cross — by sleeping.

The disciples failed. The sword wielder did not comprehend (26:51-56). The drawing of the sword is, like the sleep of the disciples, the disciples' objection to the cross. It was the last flaring-up of that passionate No to the dying Christ which had first burst forth in Peter's "God forbid, Lord!" at Caesarea Philippi. Perhaps it was a mere senseless impulse, an insane fury born of frustration that made the disciple reach for the sword even in the face of the "great crowd with swords and clubs" (26:47). But Jesus' response, "All who take the sword will perish by the sword" (26:52), is no mere general maxim; it is a judgment on all Zealotic attempts to bring on the kingdom of God by force and perhaps gives a clue to the motive behind the sword wielder's action. The sword-wielding disciple had no hope of overcoming the armed crowd singlehanded. Nor was he merely resolved to go down fighting. He was, in a sense, forcing God's hand, striking his blow in the conviction that God would not desert the man who risks his life in defense of God's Anointed — God would intervene to put the Messiah's enemies under the Messiah's feet (22:42-44; Ps. 110:1). In any case he could hardly have misunderstood the purpose of Jesus more thoroughly. Jesus wills His death; if He wanted to escape dying, He had more swords at His disposal than any Zealot could dream of providing for Him.

The disciples failed. They all fled. The words used by the evangelist exclude the possibility of conceiving this flight as a mere dispersion in panic. It was graver than that. "Then all the disciples *forsook* Him and fled" (26:56); they abandoned Him. Any last hope that Jesus might yet vindicate Himself in power, might yet at the last moment act to defend Himself and protect them, vanished now that He meekly submitted to the arrest. Jesus' words came true: "You will all fall away because of Me this night." The Shepherd is smitten and the sheep are scattered. (26:31)

The failure of the disciple goes deeper still. Peter denied his Lord (26:69-75). That Peter should have failed to keep his heroic vow, "Even if I must die with You, I will not deny You" (26:35), in such an unheroic situation as being challenged by housemaids and low-grade military is not surprising, not from any reasonable point of view; few men are capable of heroic action in ridiculous circumstances. The remarkable thing is that this failure of the "first" of the Twelve, as Matthew calls him, should have gotten into every gospel record. It is an indication not only of the unblinking veracity of that record but also, more important still, of the fact that the record is centered wholly on Jesus the Christ, who looms now in solitary majesty, now when His people reject and condemn Him and when His own, His very own, betray, forsake, and deny Him.

The cross marks the spot where the disciples failed, and it marks the spot where we all, we theologians, too, must fail. The cross marks the spot where the exegete ceases to be proud of his exegetical niceties, is shaken out of his scholarly serenity, and cries out for his life in terms of the first Beatitude. The cross marks the spot where the systematician sees his system as the instrument which focuses his failure; where the practical theologian realizes that there is only one practical thing to do, and that is to repent and abhor himself in dust and ashes; where the historian leaves his long and sanely balanced view of things and goes desperately mad. The cross marks the spot where we all become beggars — and God becomes King. Amen.

7

THE YOUNG MAN WHO FLED

(Lent)

And there followed Him a certain young man, having a linen cloth cast about his naked body, and the young men laid hold on him. And he left the linen cloth and fled from them naked.
MARK 14:51, 52

Some have supposed, and it is a very plausible supposition, that the young man mentioned in these verses is St. Mark the Evangelist himself; that St. Mark is here putting his signature to his gospel. If that is so, St. Mark is recording his own shame, and he is not the only inspired writer to do so. The early church has preserved for us the tradition that the Gospel According to St. Mark is the record of the preaching of St. Peter, who in his preaching obviously did not spare himself. The Gospel that reflects his preaching is as unsparing as any in its portrayal of his weaknesses, his misunderstandings, and his denial; in fact it omits some things creditable to St. Peter which St. Matthew records. St. Paul himself, too, tells us that he persecuted the church, and does so that he may glorify the grace of his Lord the more. St. Mark, then, belongs to that goodly fellowship who sought not their own glory but Another's, who had lost themselves in the wonder

46

of the forgiving love of the God who had met them in Jesus, who is the Christ. What they write is not of themselves or for themselves. It is written for our learning.

The young man who fled learned something important that night on which, whether from youthful curiosity or whatever motive, he followed Jesus and His disciples from afar when they left the Upper Room for the Garden of Gethsemane. He wanted to look on, to see what would happen. He learned that you cannot be a spectator of the Lord Jesus Christ; you cannot follow from a distance and look on. You are involved one way or another as soon as you confront Him.

He had learned the lesson, partly at least. The full lesson did not come easy, not even for the men whom we now call Saints with a capital "S." The young man, John Mark, had promise. St. Paul took him along on the missionary journey, the first one, that was to carry him through Cyprus and into Asia Minor. St. Mark did well enough on Cyprus apparently, amid the familiar pattern of his Jewish life, in the preaching in the synagog of the Diaspora. But on the starkly Gentile coasts of Asia Minor his courage failed him once more, and again he sought to follow his Lord from afar, as a spectator, from his mother's house in Jerusalem. When Barnabas wished to take him along on the second missionary journey, St. Paul objected so violently that he and Barnabas quarreled and separated. Barnabas took his cousin Mark and went once more to Cyprus. We lose sight of him for some years after that. Somewhere in those years he learned those lessons fully. When next we hear of him, he is a fellow worker and a comfort to that fighter of the good fight, St. Paul, who bespeaks a welcome for him from the good people of Colossae. And when, again some years later, St. Paul summons Timothy to Rome that he may see him before he dies, he bids Timothy bring Mark with him and pays him the good workman's tribute: "For he is profitable to me for the ministry." The Christian who could thus confidently be summoned to Rome to be present at the execution of a Christian, not without risk to himself, had ceased to be a spectator and had become a witness. Except for an affectionate word from St. Peter we know nothing more of him. Later tradition has it that he made a good end and witnessed with his blood to the Lord, whose life he found the grace to pen.

The Lord Jesus Christ wants no spectators; St. Mark has taught us this in these two verses. We learn it everywhere in Scripture. Zacchaeus, who "sought to see Jesus who He was," was not allowed to remain in this spectator's perch in the sycamore tree. Jesus confronted him, and confronted him with a decision: "Make haste and come down, for today I must abide at thy house." The Lord Jesus Christ tolerates no spectators. You are either for Him, or you are against Him. He not only hung on the cross in space between two malefactors; He drew a sharp furrow of life and death between them. The one reviled Him; the other said, "Remember Thou me!"

This lesson comes hard to our comfortable Christianity. We six-to-the-padded-pew disiciples have blurred the line of the either-or; we grow uneasy at the fact, the completely obvious fact, that if we are involved with Jesus Christ at all, we are totally involved. "With the *heart* man believeth," and "heart" in Biblical language is the whole man — his mind, his feelings, his will, and all that is within him. If some cynical joker, disgusted at our parochial squabbling, were to write over the church door, "Fighting Room Only," he would be telling the sober truth albeit unconsciously. To believe on the Lord Jesus Christ does not mean only that we have become acquainted with a "catechismful" of facts about Him; it means that we have been drawn into the live momentum of a life that was lived to destroy the works of the devil. And there *is* fighting room only. "Fight the good fight of faith, lay hold on eternal life" is not just something that lends solemn pathos to the confirmation service; it is written over our whole life. Every minute brings a decision for or against Christ, and the decision involves a struggle and a fight.

If this begins to sound like overstrained rhetoric, let us put it to the test of fact. What happened the last time we were in church? When "In the name of the Father and of the Son and of the Holy Ghost" was pronounced to us, we were in the presence of almighty God. How long did we stay there? Did we loll our way through the Common Service, or did we fight our way through, making the hard decisions against the distractions from within and without? Did we confess our sins, or did we recite the Confession of Sins and pass off our wrong decision, the decision not to trouble ourselves too much this morning about the Lord Jesus Christ but blame the "cold formalism" of the liturgy, that beating heart of Christendom? Did we fight for the Word, resisting the enemy, who is always on the snatch for it, or did we let it roll over us? Were we spectators or were we *there,* with the Lord Jesus Christ?

Whether we put it into words or not, most of us believe in our hearts that the decision was somehow easier in the heroic days when there were stakes to be burned at and lions to be thrown to. Our days are soundproofed against leonine roarings, and our temperatures are a genteel and uniform 72, thermostatically controlled. Perhaps; but the noises would grow, and the temperature would rise if we began making some little decisions, on the spot, like not letting the next dirty story pass; like not smiling indulgently or joining in, the next bit of greasy anti-Semitism that meets us, or the next calm and deadly cold assumption that the Negro is the inferior of the white man. Or we might try telling the next mealy moralist we meet, the next "do well, and all's well" gentleman that strikes up a "religious" conversation with us, the whole bitter truth, for his good. — Life would not be so simple anymore, but it would be a Christian life, with the first syllable, "Christ," spelled out upon it, and we should cease being spectators and become witnesses ready for the lions and the stakes, if they come. Amen.

8

THE ROYAL BANNERS FORWARD GO, I

(Lent)

But what think ye? A certain man had two sons, and he came to the first and said, Son, go work today in my vineyard. He answered and said, I will not; but afterward he repented and went. And he came to the second and said likewise. And he answered and said, I go, sir, and went not. Whether of them twain did the will of his father? They say unto Him, The first. Jesus saith unto them, Verily I say unto you that the publicans and the harlots go into the kingdom of God before you. For John came unto you in the way of righteousness, and ye believed him not, but the publicans and the harlots believed him. And ye, when ye had seen it, repented not afterward, that ye might believe him. — MATTHEW 21:28-32

"The royal banners forward go; the cross shines forth in mystic glow." The meek King goes to the cross. His banners summon His people to repentance, and they call on us. How do we salute those banners? How do we acclaim that Victor-Servant? How do we serve that King? The words which Jesus spoke can serve us and help us find an answer to our question. They can help us, that is, if we remember that all those terrible things that happened in the week before Good Friday recur — in respectable, Christianized form of

51

course — in the years after Good Friday. Let us not spend
a comfortable Lententide denouncing Jesus' contemporaries.
That would not be keeping a true Lent; that would not be
a fast, for people we feel superior to make mighty good
eating. That would be

> to quit the dish
> of flesh and still
> to fill
> the platter high with fish.

Let us hear *Jesus' word to the dodgers, the evaders,* and
see how it applies to us. The word which the Father speaks
in this parable reminds Israel once more of all God's ancient mercy to His people. It is a summary of the whole
Old Testament:

"Son, Go Work Today in My Vineyard."

"Son" — the whole grace of God's covenant love for His
people is in this word: "When Israel was young, then did
I love him, and out of Egypt did I call My son." "Go
work today" — the Lord's claim upon His people, the fact
that He desired the whole man wholly for Himself, appears
in these words — "Thou shalt love the Lord, thy God, with
all thy heart." And the inescapable urgency of God's claim
is spoken once more in "today." "In *My* vineyard" — the
whole scene of man's work and man's history is the Lord's,
under His governance. The Creator God, the sovereign Lord
of all history, appears in this word. All the grace and power
of God that made Israel the Sabbath among the nations
appears once more in the words which bid the son give
God a son's devotion and render Him a son's service.

We all know what the men of Jesus' generation answered.
The young man said, "I go, sir," and went not. Let us not
paint this young man too black. He represents the best in
Israel. He did not become a hellion. He did not disgrace

his parents and squander his patrimony. He did not look on the wine when it was red or consort with loose women. No (and this is what makes this such an embarrassing text to preach on just here), our young man pursued wisdom. He became a churchman and a theologian. He probably attended *Leb Echad* (that's a very rough rendering of *Concordia*) Seminary.

Our young man cultivated the liturgical life. He fasted, he tithed, he prayed, and he washed. Jesus' contemporaries were probably the fastingest, the tithingest, the prayingest, the ablutingest generation of men under the sun. Moreover, our young man developed an intense missionary activity; he compassed sea and land to make one proselyte. He became a theologian and discussed a whole mess of problems. We are not the first generation of theologians to discuss a wide variety of "The Church *and*" themes. Our young man had them and discussed them too. He had his *The Church and Society,* his theological-sociological problems. He was interested in almsgiving, in the right reasons for a valid divorce, and he was interested in the supreme question too, the question, Who is my neighbor? He had his *The Church and Government* problem too, his theological-political problem, and he asked, Is it lawful to pay tax to Caesar? *The Church and the Bible* was in his life too; he had his theological-exegetical problem, and he asked, Which is the greatest commandment? He was seeking an integrating principle for a truly Biblical theology.

What was it that made our demure young theologian-churchman an abomination? What made his converts sons of Gehenna? Why did the publicans and harlots go into the Kingdom before him? Where did he fail? *He went not.* He remained rooted in himself, cabined, cribbed, confined, bound in by his own religiosity, by his liturgy, his theology. He dis-

cussed and groped and fiddled with his problems; he evaded.
For our young man knew in his heart of hearts (what we
know too) that once we understand and admit that we understand, then we must obey. Then there is only one problem, one that we can't walk around anymore, one that we
can't discuss anymore. This one problem always confronts
us head on. Once we know that there is really no problem
like "Who is my neighbor?" and that finding him is not only
easy but inevitable; once we face up to the fact that we
must take steps if we want to avoid our neighbor, that our
neighbor is always lying across our path — then there is
only one problem left; then we must love our neighbor as
ourselves.

John the Baptist made plain to his contemporaries that
there is only one problem because there is only one God and
that one God is drawing near in the person of His Son and
Servant, the Mightier One. There is only one road to go:
the road of repentance. The unproblematical publicans and
the nonliturgical harlots believed John the Baptist. But
what of our evading theologian? "Ye repented not afterward, that ye might believe him."

Theologians find it hard to repent; they do not often
repent. They improve their theology; they rethink their
position. They modify their views in the light of new
discoveries; they peer into hot caves and find new materials
for cool disputings. They take into account of course the
epoch-making work of the great Dr. Gedankenspritzer. For
whatever you may think of the great Dr. Gedankenspritzer,
you cannot simply ignore him. (It is academic heresy to
say so, but the heretical thought *will* rise, Why *not,* for a
change, ignore the current Dr. Gedankenspritzer? It might
be a good thing, even for Dr. Gedankenspritzer.)

Jesus loved even the churchmen and the theologians, even

the disobedient sons. For us theological sons and for our salvation He was made man. The one obedient Son, the Son who had only one problem, to do the will of the Father who sent Him, He *lived* by the Word that proceeded from the mouth of God and went in free obedience the way which that Word marked for Him, the way to the cross. He redeemed the ruin of our broken "I go, Sir." We live by His blood outpoured. He has broken open a path to the vineyard of God for us, a path that we can walk because He has walked it before us and for us. Our liturgy, our activity, our theology need no longer be gifts of God that we use against God to evade Him. Let us face it. This can happen here; this has happened here. But it need not happen here. Our liturgy, our activity, our theology, yea, even the work of the great Dr. Gedankenspritzer can be a part of our work today in the vineyard of our Father. For the Cross, the royal banner of our King, blazons forth both: "Son, thy sins be forgiven thee," and

"Son, go work today in My vineyard." Amen.

THE ROYAL BANNERS FORWARD GO, II

Hear another parable: There was a certain householder which planted a vineyard, and hedged it round about, and digged a winepress in it, and built a tower, and let it out to husbandmen, and went into a far country. And when the time of the fruit drew near, he sent his servants to the husbandmen that they might receive the fruits of it. And the husbandmen took his servants and beat one and killed another and stoned another. Again, he sent other servants more than the first, and they did unto them likewise. But last of all he sent unto them his son, saying, They will reverence my son. But when the husbandmen saw the son, they said among themselves: This is the heir. Come, let us kill him, and let us seize on his inheritance. And they caught him and cast him out of the vineyard and slew him. When the lord therefore of the vineyard cometh, what will he do unto those husbandmen? They say unto him, He will miserably destroy those wicked men and will let out his vineyard unto other husbandmen, which shall render him the fruits in their seasons. Jesus saith unto them, Did ye never read in the Scriptures: The Stone which the builders rejected, the same is become the Head of the corner; this is the Lord's doing, and it is marvelous in our eyes? Therefore say I unto you, The kingdom of God shall be taken from you and given to a nation bringing forth the fruits thereof. — MATTHEW 21:33-43

The royal banners forward go; they summon God's sons, and the sons evade the summons. They call on God's workmen, His tenant farmers, to give God the fruits of His vineyard, and God's workmen rebel.

Jesus' Word to the Rebels: "Give God What Is God's!"

That is an old cry, a cry that spans 28 centuries. Isaiah raised that cry; Jesus raised it; and in our 20th century it must be raised again. Isaiah pictured to his generation the free and fostering love of God that chose out Israel to be His pleasant plant: God planted His vineyard in the best soil, on the best site (on a hill where grapes may drink the sun), and gave it the best cultivation. He looked, therefore, to find noble grapes — and found wild grapes. He looked to Israel to find there a rule of right — and found in His people the misrule of might. (Isaiah 5)

"What could have been done *more* to my vineyard . . . ?" Israel's history is the record of that miracle of miracles, the "more" of God, that inexplicable onward march of the Lord's love for His people, that impetus of God which finally made His royal banner the cross. That "more" is documented in the servants of the Lord, those waves on waves of prophets who proffered Israel God's grace and bade Israel give God what is God's. That "more" reaches its climax in the sending of the Son: "They will reverence My Son." There is the apex of that love of God, love with defenses down, love that risks betrayal, lost love to the loveless shown.

This is the ultimate grace, the culminating revelation. And it provokes the ultimate rebellion: "This is the Heir; let us kill Him, and let us seize on His inheritance." These keepers of the vineyard saw clearly, up to a point at least. With the stupid clarity of demonic vision they saw this: If we get rid of the Son, *we'll* be in charge: *we'll* have it made. The prophets are dead; we can always reinterpret them to suit our ends and thus stone them anew. But the Son lives and confronts us. His greatness makes us bow. His obedience indicts us in our rebelliousness. He summons us, inexorably, to give God what is God's.

They got rid of the Son. They caught Him, cast Him out of the vineyard, and slew Him. They got rid of the Son, but they could not seize on His inheritance. They lost the vineyard, and the Stone which they rejected became the rock that ground them to powder. — But there was another chapter of God's love written before that chapter of doom. The Son loved these rebels. Christ interceded for them and died for them. When He arose, He sent His messengers first to them. He let His servants Stephen, James, the son of Zebedee, and James the Just die in their witness to them.

Such is our Christ, a Christ who died for rebels. Do *we* qualify as rebels, now, in this year of *our Lord?* Can it happen here? Can it be that we drag the Heir out of the vineyard and seek to take over? Our Lord foresaw that it could happen. Salt that does not salt, light that does not shine, workmen who will not give the Lord of the vineyard His fruit — these are three of a kind, all highly "unnatural," all rebellion against God, who creates salt, gives light, and makes men His workmen.

It can happen here; it has happened. The heresies of which we read in the apostolic writings are, all of them, attempts to get the Heir out of the vineyard, attempts to remove the Son and to leave the workmen in charge. The men who strove to make a fair show in the flesh in Galatia; the men in Colossae who restored to honor the principalities and powers which the Christ had spoiled; Cerinthus with his Christ who came by water but not by blood, essentially an uncrucified Christ; the Christ party at Corinth (how neatly the rebellion can disguise itself!) who rose to heights of religion's self-fulfillment and left behind and below them the apostle who knew only the Crucified — they all "revised" the Christ whom God had given. And every "revised" Christ is a Christ dragged out of the vineyard and slain. For this revised

Christ is no longer the Son whose obedience indicts us; He is no longer the Christ whose ransoming cross spells out our bankruptcy.

The Christ, the obedient Son, the Crucified, comes to us still. He comes to us in the Word of His apostles. His presence is a real presence — in a book, a presence as offensive as His presence in the flesh, as offensive as His presence in the bread and wine. When we play off the Christ against the Book, His Book; when we leave the Book and wander out behind the beyond, seeking His presence behind and beyond the Book, we are nudging the real Christ out of the vineyard. We destroy the Heir by excision and revision.

We can destroy the Heir by substitution also. When we play off His Word against His sacrament or His sacrament against His Word, let's not delude ourselves about what is going on. It is the same ugly business as that recorded in Matthew 21:33-43. And it is the same ugly business when we set an autonomous *Wissenschaft* over His Word, or a philosophy, or a system; when we substitute a set of principles for the living Lord; when we make of His sacrament our sacrifice, etc., etc., etc.

We cannot destroy the Heir. But we can destroy ourselves. But we need not destroy ourselves. What can happen after Good Friday, what has happened with an ugly repetitiousness since Good Friday, that need not happen here. The Son and Heir has made us God's pleasant plant; He has made us branches of that one vine whose fruit was all for God. When He comes to us in the Word of His apostles, we can hear Him speaking to us still and can submit to Him in the obedience of faith. When He comes to us in the bread and wine and the cry goes up, "Lift up your hearts," we can, in the powers of our communion with Him, reply: "We lift them up unto the Lord." Amen.

THE ROYAL BANNERS FORWARD GO, III

And Jesus answered and spake unto them again by parables and said: The kingdom of heaven is like unto a certain king which made a marriage for his son, and sent forth his servants to call them that were bidden to the wedding, and they would not come. Again he sent forth other servants, saying: Tell them which are bidden, Behold, I have prepared my dinner. My oxen and my fatlings are killed, and all things are ready. Come unto the marriage. But they made light of it and went their ways, one to his farm, another to his merchandise. And the remnant took his servants and entreated them spitefully and slew them. But when the king heard thereof, he was wroth, and he sent forth his armies and destroyed those murderers and burned up their city. Then saith he to his servants: The wedding is ready, but they which were bidden were not worthy. Go ye therefore into the highways, and as many as ye shall find, bid to the marriage. So those servants went out into the highways and gathered together all as many as they found, both bad and good, and the wedding was furnished with guests. And when the king came in to see the guests, he saw there a man which had not on a wedding garment. And he saith unto him, Friend, how comest thou in hither not having a wedding garment? And he was speechless. Then said the king to the servants: Bind him hand and foot and take him away and cast him into outer darkness; there shall be weeping and gnashing of teeth. For many are called, but few are chosen. — MATTHEW 22:1-14

The royal banners forward go. They summon God's sons, and the sons evade. They summon God's workmen, and the workmen rebel. They bid God's guests come to the wedding feast, and the guests despise that bidding.

Jesus' Word to the Contemptuous Guests

The royal banners forward go. And the device upon those banners is *grace*. It is royal grace, grace bestowed in sovereign freedom, a grace which one cannot induce, cannot claim, cannot compel. One can only receive it. You *get* invited to the King's wedding supper.

It is festal grace, splendid, lavish, extravagant, prodigal. Everybody spends too much on weddings, and so it is just wedding festivity that furnishes the figure for the grace of God. *"All* things are ready; come unto the marriage!"

It is calling, inviting grace with a repeated urgent, seeking, and unwearied call. This King will have His chambers filled with guests, no matter what.

It is absolute grace, pure grace, and therefore it is universal grace. This grace invites "both bad and good." This pretty well covers mankind. No one is excepted; no one is excluded. Only those who refuse this grace prove "unworthy" of it.

And it is personal grace. "The king came in to see the guests" — that is the climax and the meaning of the feast, personal communion, face to face. To him who has abused this grace the King says, *"Friend,* how camest thou hither?"

"Dies Evangelium ist nicht schwer," Luther says. The royal banners forward go, and any fool can read what is emblazoned on them. "Und ist ein schrecklich Evangelium," he goes on. What makes this Gospel "schrecklich"? Why does the lighted banquet hall have as its foil the outer darkness where there is weeping and gnashing of teeth? Why do our Lord's progressing banners leave behind them the bodies of men lying on the streets of their burnt and ruined city?

Nothing is so sure, so wholly sure, so surely sure as God in the giving of His grace. Nothing is so unsure, so fearfully precarious as our hold upon that grace. Therefore the whole New Testament is filled with faith and fear, with jubilance and trembling, because of this dark mystery of our manhood, the mystery whereof the prophet spoke: "Wherefore do ye spend money for that which is not bread?" We all know, theoretically, that "there is none good but one, that is, God." And yet we decide, practically, that some pelting farm or some mincing merchandise is better than that good, that is, right now at least, *pro tem.* And so we "make light" of the inviting God, despise His invitation, and do away with His messengers. That despised and desecrated grace becomes a treasury of wrath against the Day of Wrath and the righteous judgment of God.

Our Lord speaks also of another, subtler form of making light of God's inviting grace when He speaks of the man who came to the wedding but came without the wedding garment. We all know, theoretically and in general, that God's grace is not something like a bucket of paint in a corner that we can use from time to time to make our black fences white. We know that the King's grace is a personal grace, one that has both enriched us *and* claimed us. We know that the high majesty of God is in that grace, in fact, is that grace. And we know that we not only *have* that grace but also live by it, must live by it if we are to live at all. But for practical purposes and for the time being we live as if (that diabolical "as if") — as if that grace were separable from God, as if we could hear the Word that proceeds from the mouth of God and not live by it, as if we could pray half of the Fifth Petition. And so we take our chances on appearing at God's banquet in a robe of our own wearing, in a tissue of lies. We take our chances on hearing that terrible word *"Friend,* how camest thou hither?"

The royal banners forward go. This is not a parade that we may watch. The banners summon us, God's sons, God's workmen, God's guests. We have the fearful freedom, the freedom to evade, to rebel, to despise. But no; we do not really have it. The Son has set us free from that fatal freedom; He has set us free for God. Amen.

9

THE BEATING HEART OF ALL OUR HOPE

(Easter)

Now if Christ be preached that He rose from the dead, how say some among you that there is no resurrection of the dead? But if there be no resurrection of the dead, then is Christ not risen. And if Christ be not risen, then is our preaching vain, and your faith is also vain. Yea, and we are found false witnesses of God because we have testified of God that He raised up Christ, whom He raised not up, if so be that the dead rise not. For if the dead rise not, then is not Christ raised. And if Christ be not raised, your faith is vain; ye are yet in your sins. Then they also which are fallen asleep in Christ are perished. If in this life only we have hope in Christ, we are of all men most miserable. But now is Christ risen from the dead and become the firstfruits of them that slept. For since by man came death, by man came also the resurrection of the dead. For as in Adam all die, even so in Christ shall all be made alive.

1 CORINTHIANS 15:12-22

The church at Corinth was the first in history to be infiltrated by liberalism. It was a brilliant, persuasive kind of liberalism, thoroughgoing, self-willed, and audacious. It swung wide and cut deep.

Paul's whole First Letter to the Corinthians attests how widely and radically this liberalism affected the whole life of the Christians of Corinth. The line between the church of God at Corinth and the Greek world in Corinth was being very faintly drawn.

And so it is not surprising to find that the Christian belief which was most offensive to the Greek mind, the bodily resurrection of the dead, was being sacrificed to Greek sensibilities. The new liberals at Corinth found it an expendable piece of theology, and since it "kept the Greeks out of the church," they let it go. They did not deny the resurrection of Jesus from the dead, but they no longer affirmed that His resurrection was significant for all men, the living and the dead. To meet, challenge, and destroy this piece of liberal accommodation to Greek thinking, Paul wrote the great 15th chapter of First Corinthians.

The liberals moved with supple versatility in the world of ideas. Paul does not go down to meet them in their dim and airless world; he hauls them out into his own bright apostolic world, the world of the Gospel, and confronts them with a fact. He confronts them with that act of God which dealt effectually with man's sins: Christ died for our sin (*our s*ins — this is an event that involves us all), was buried, and rose again the third day, "according to the Scriptures" — it was the counsel and the will of God that He should so die and so rise again.

This is not a malleable idea but a rock-hard fact. The Law required two or three witnesses to a fact, and Paul duly calls his witnesses, twice three sets of them, in number more than 500; most of them, moreover, still live and can tell. Paul himself is among these living witnesses. The risen Christ appeared to him and made the persecutor of the church His messenger, His apostle. Paul experienced the resurrection of Jesus Christ as the huge and incredible grace of God, the grace which reversed the whole current of his life and set him on that toilsome apostolic course which carried him to Corinth.

The resurrection of Jesus Christ is therefore something quite outside and independent of the thinking and willing of man; it is not any man's idea but God's act. As God's act it is the content of the apostolic preachment — Paul's and all the apostles' — and the content of the faith of the men of Corinth. This act of God sets them on their feet; this act of God delivers them from death. Only under this sky of divine forgiveness can men breathe eternal air.

It was *Christ* who died, and it was *Christ* who rose. That means One died for all and rose for all, for when God acted in Christ, He acted for all the world; He was reconciling the *world* to Himself. Therefore the resurrection of Christ and the resurrection of the dead stand and fall together. To affirm the one is to affirm the other, and to deny the one is to deny the other.

The Corinthian liberals had denied the resurrection of the dead; Paul makes plain to them what they have thereby denied (vv. 12-19): "If you deny the resurrection of the dead, if you abandon your dead to death, you are saying no less than this: 'God has not, after all, dealt effectually with our sins; the blank and beetling wall of death has not been pierced after all; Christ never broke through that wall, and there is no passing through it now.' You are saying that your Christ is dead. Your Christ is dead, and so our preaching is empty, and your faith is vain."

And if Christ is dead, then the apostolic preaching has lost all point and purpose; an apostle of Jesus Christ cannot go up and down the Roman roads delivering lectures on a dead hero; he must be able to preach a Gospel of life and proclaim a living Lord.

Faith, too, has lost its content; a noble martyr executed

by the Romans in Jerusalem is not the divine answer to the fatal question of man's sin and provides no content for the faith of man. The Christian hope, too, has then become a delusion, a cruel lie which cheats men of the present life, the only life they can look to have.

"But now is Christ risen from the dead," and the resurrection of Christ determines all things from this time forth and forever (vv. 20-28). The great deed of God is done, and it cannot be undone again. It is fact, and the fact is significant; it controls the future. The risen Christ is the "Firstfruits of them that slept" — He is the first ripe Grain on the field, the Token and the Guarantee of the harvest which God will gather wholly into His barns.

His resurrection is the first and decisive blast of God's great final music. That music cannot cease because the score is written by God, and He writes no unfinished symphonies. As surely as Adam once set a fatal deathward cadence for mankind and made all human life a march of death, so surely has Christ reversed that cadence and made it a music that shall surge inevitably upward to eternal life. The risen Son of God must reign; He shall go His way of ministry to the utmost end until all enemies are put under His feet, even the last enemy, death, until He presents to the Father a Son's obeisance and a Son's gift: a world made wholly God's again, a world in which divine life triumphs and the living God is All in all.

Paul has spelled out the significance of the resurrection both negatively (vv. 12-19) and positively (vv. 20-28); but he has not yet exhausted that significance. For the resurrection affects not only preaching, faith, and hope; it determines the whole bent and temper of our lives, our conduct. And it is to this that Paul now turns. (Vv. 29-34)

Suppose there is no resurrection of the dead, what then?

"What shall they do who are baptized for the dead if the dead rise not at all?" Interpreters have puzzled over this verse in vain. Paul was no doubt alluding to something familiar to both his readers and himself, but it escapes us. In the light of the sentences which follow it would seem that Paul is referring to some form of self-sacrificing Christian ministry, one that involved suffering and dying — "baptism" is used occasionally as a figure for suffering and death. (Mark 10:38)

How shall Paul continue in his ministry if the dead rise not at all? (Vv. 30-32) His ministry is one in which he faces death and danger constantly. He is like a gladiator fighting wild beasts in the arena. He is a professional in enduring danger and in facing death. And what for? If this life be all the life he has, if he cannot work and endure in the conviction that his "light affliction, which is but for a moment, worketh . . . a far more exceeding and eternal weight of glory" (2 Cor. 4:17), he would be better advised to eat and drink and live at ease and die when die he must.

Paul is dead serious about this, far more serious than his brilliant opponents. They are entertaining a new theological idea or developing a new theological approach and really do not expect anyone to draw such stiff conclusions from their fluid premises. "Be not deceived," Paul tells them, "you cannot fill yourselves with these ideas, and you cannot fill the air with this talk without corrupting men — yourselves and others. You are making feeble and afraid the gladiators of God, and you are intoxicating yourselves." He bids them sober up (v. 34); that is what the word translated with "awake" means literally. For men who have heard and believed the good news of the risen Christ to deny the resurrection of the dead is to be drunk, adrift in a vague and illusory world of their own fancies, out of touch with reality, out of touch with the fact that determines all reality, all history, and all men's lives. Paul concludes by reproaching the men who prided themselves on their "knowledge" — knowledge which is really ignorance — ignorance of God, who is God of the living, not of the dead.

Men trust their own brains more than they trust God. When they are faced with what overtowers their conceiving, they conclude: "What I cannot understand or explain cannot be." The Corinthians objected to the resurrection of the dead because they could not understand how a dead and disintegrated body could be restored to wholeness and life. They therefore raised the skeptical question: *"How are the dead raised?"* The question is evidence of their ignorance of God, and Paul therefore calls it a fool's question, that is, the question of one who cannot or will not see what God has set before his eyes. They are men of little faith, and that makes them men of little vision too. Little faith can become great faith only when confronted by the greatness of God, who is the Object of faith.

Paul turns these people from their brains to God and bids them consider Him, the Creator, whose creative possibilities know no limits. The wells of God have never yet gone dry, as even a fool can see if he will take the trouble to look around him at the prodigal and varied splendor of God's working in the world. One glance anywhere in the world, and the eye of faith beholds the prolific splendor of the Lord of life documented in a thousand ways (vv. 36-41). His almighty, creative working can overclothe our corruption with incorruption, our disfigurement with glory, our weakness with strength. He who has given us earthly bodies can give us spiritual bodies, bodies which are the fit and perfect instrument of the new man, in whom the Spirit dwells. He who dressed us in the earthly dress of Adam can clothe us in Christ. Whether we be among those in the grave or among the living at the coming of Christ, God, who created the new and eternal world, will fit us and dress us for that brave new world. The dead shall be raised incorruptible, and the living shall be transfigured, in the twinkling of an eye, when the trumpet sounds.

Paul ends where he began, with the fact that God has dealt triumphantly with the sin of man. That is the beating heart of all our hope, the sure and solid basis of our triumph over death. For it was sin that made death strong; sin was death's "sting," the goad with which death hearded us home, his dumb and doomed and driven cattle. Now we can sing:

> O Death, where is thy sting?
> O Grave, where is thy victory?

And now we can work. Paul's meeting with the risen Christ set him to work; his witness to the risen Christ sets us to work. With a firm and solid stance on this territory of triumph we can work the work of the Lord, assured that what we build for Him will never fall. Amen.

10

THE WAITING BRIDE OF CHRIST

(Whitsunday)

And the Spirit and the bride say, Come. And let him that heareth say, Come. And let him that is athirst come. And whosoever will, let him take the water of life freely.

REVELATION 22:17

I believe in the Holy Ghost. . . . And I believe one holy Christian and apostolic church. . . . And I look for . . . the life of the world to come.

These three belong together: the Holy Spirit, the church, and the hope of the world to come — one Spirit, one body, one hope of your calling. The church, the waiting bride of Christ, is a fit subject for our contemplation on Pentecost, the Feast of the Holy Ghost. Her song, "Come" is a fit subject for our singing.

Oh, come,

Thou Son of Man, who walkest amid the candle-
sticks,

Whose eye is on the church,

O Thou, girt in splendor and robed in magnificent
mercy,

Come!

O Thou Lamb of God that wast slain, Thou that
    openest the seals of Thy Father's book,
Thou Lord of all happenings on earth —
Let the last riders of destruction ride their dread-
    ful last —
Oh, come!
O Thou Rider upon the white horse,
Thou Overcomer of all opposing hosts,
O Thou Lord of lords and King of kings,
Oh, come, take up Thy power and reign!
Send out Thine angel armies into every highway,
    road, and lane,
Out into every hot and steaming pavement and all
    the stinking alleys of our world,
And make them cool and sweet and pleasant path-
    ways for Thy feet.
Send out Thy re-creating angels, and let them shout
    for joy and take up the song of the primeval
    "Very Good!" once more.
Send Thy cleansing couriers out through every field
    and wood, and put the first morning's dew
    on every branch and leaf again.
Set free the groaning creation, set all free —
Till every little bird twitches his tail in ecstasy,
A living metronome for the angelic and unending
    Alleluias of the world to come.
Oh, come!

Such meditation and such song would be altogether seemly,
altogether comely, in this Whitsuntide.

But we are being interrupted. Here comes Freiherr von
Aktivismus with his company. Here are Messrs. Here and
Now (both muttering, "Let us have no eschatological non-

sense, please!"); here are Mr. Research and Mr. Statistics, Mr. Graphs and Mr. Charts, Mr. Extrapolation, Mr. Civic Consciousness — and to give the proceedings the benefit of her patrician air, Her Grace, the Countess of Misericordia Cum Lacrimis Effusis. They have an indictment against the waiting bride, and they will make short shrift with her. The trial will be a mere formality. They have a branding iron hot and ready to impress upon her clear and innocent brow. They will brand her with a capital Q, for she is guilty of quietism!

Who will save the waiting bride? Who will appear in defense of her song? Let St. Paul appear for the defense; he is an apostle and knows a thing or two about the apostolic church.

"When my Lord sent me out into the cities of the Gentiles to raise up churches for His glory there," St. Paul says, "He bade me build into their lives a triple movement, a triple beat. I bade men

> turn from idols;
> serve the true and living God;
> wait for His Son from heaven . . . even
> Jesus, who delivers us from the wrath to come.
> (1 Thess. 1:9, 10)

Let no one dare to change this triple beat; let no one presume to shorten it to two — all three are necessary to the life and health of the church, all are indispensable. I could tell you a sad story of what happened in Corinth when the church no longer said, "Come!" What harlotries men practiced with their bodies when they forgot that these bodies were to be resurrected bodies.

"Moreover, Freiherr von Aktivismus, if you had not been so wrapped up with your graphs and your statistics, so ready and so eager with your capital Q, you might have considered *who* is singing, 'Come.' This is the Spirit singing. If you want activity, have a look at Him. He has been active since creation, active in history, rousing up a Gideon, for instance, more potent than the men and horses of Egypt; He spake by the prophets — it was one of these men of the Spirit who was moved by Him to say, 'I will have mercy and not sacrifice.' Men full of the *Spirit* and wisdom looked after the widows and the fatherless in the Jerusalem church.

"It is the bride of Christ who sings, bone of His bone, flesh of His flesh, willing His will, the will of Him who said, 'My Father worketh hitherto, and I work.'

"You might have considered also, Freiherr, to whom they are saying, 'Come! They are crying to Christ, who says,

> Behold, I come quickly,
> and My reward is with Me,
> to give every man *according as his work shall be.*

They are invoking Judgment Day with their song.

"You might have noted also, all you capital Q gentry, *how* the inspired bride says, 'Come!' She is inviting all men to join in the cry: 'Let him that heareth say, Come! And whosoever will, let him take the water of life freely.' If you had not been so proud of your tears, Countess Misericordia, you might have noted: She is not wallowing in her hope; she lives by it. She who is ready to share the water of life will give more mundane waters too. This dainty bride, this single-hearted and highhearted girl, will have washed a dozen dirty babies and have kissed them too while you, Freiherr, are gathering statistics on the incidence of babies that need washing. While you, countess, weep hot salt tears, she will have given fresh water and cool to thirsty travelers." So far St. Paul.

"Travelers" — we cannot forget, if we live in the rhythm

of St. Paul's triple beat, that our charity to travelers: drink to travelers on their way to Canaan, in the wilderness; food to travelers in the wilderness; tents for travelers in the wilderness, *tents* that they can strike and travel on again. If we stop singing, "Come," our well-intentioned charity will trap men in the wilderness. We shall build air-conditioned housing units in the wilderness, built to last a thousand years. Look at them — who would ever want to leave them? — each unit with a balcony looking toward Egypt affording a fine view of the fleshpots.

When the church no longer cries, "Come!" when the church no longer looks to the end, then means become ends; that is, they become idols from which we can no longer turn to serve the living God. Take this fine thing with the ominous name, the church's "image"; the church that has forgotten her coming Lord will worship her own "image" instead of her Lord.

Or let us move in close to home, to our theology. What happens to exegesis, when exegesis no longer says, "Maranatha!"? Exegesis can become an autonomous *Wissenschaft,* a cerebral Vanity Fair complete with merry-go-rounds of exegetical fads, with cunningly constructed mazes of conjectures and hypotheses, with contending calliopes that fill the air and intoxicate the senses, but do not say, He cometh, He cometh to judge the earth," and do not shout, "Lift up your hearts!"

When liturgics forgets that all worship is waiting for the Lord, then we begin to worship our worship and to adore our adorations; then we begin to genuflect before encrusted chasubles and play the harlot under every green tree with esthetically selected traditions.

But where the Spirit is, there is liberty. He sets us free, free from idols, free to serve the living God. He gives us a

high hope that sets us free from ourselves, from grim intro-
spection and fruitless preoccupation with our own religious
psychology. He sets us free, not least, for praise. So let us
forget that hot and searing capital Q. Let us sing a little and
live — and serve — a lot. Amen.

11

POOR IN SPIRIT

(Installation of Professor of Old Testament Interpretation)

Blessed are the poor in spirit, for theirs is the kingdom of heaven.
MATTHEW 5:3

You are this afternoon being installed in the office to which you have been duly called, that of professor of theology. In such a solemn moment as this it behooves us all to bethink ourselves and to consider what the basic fact of being a theologian is, for every man that professes Christianity is a theologian in the ancient and honorable, the original, sense of that word. He is a herald and proclaimer of the God in whom he believes. And for the true theologian, the theologian of the theology of the cross, the first Beatitude is a text to cast light upon the nature and the work of such a theologian of the cross.

Now, every theologian has before him two choices. Either he can cast a critical and selective eye upon God's revelation of Himself, upon Scripture, and according to his own preferences and predilections make his God of whatever elements in that revelation seem to him essential and "of abiding value." He can reject, select, trim, splice, plane, and smoothe

77

according to his bent and bias and build himself a comfortable, medium-size deity with whom he can stand pretty well shoulder to shoulder, a god who will not dwarf him overmuch, a god who can reasonably be expected even to feel flattered that someone believes in him. If a man chooses to be a theologian of that sort, he can still loom quite magnificently against the sky in the full stature of the autonomous man as man would naturally like to be. He can live out his days in a kind of bland and self-sufficient security. To be sure, the great and persistent question of "the valley of the shadow of death," that inescapable mote to trouble the mind's eye, will remain unanswered. But what of that? Is not our brave, clever little man a theologian? Does he not write books? And do not people read and review them and find them — bless the mark — "stimulating and suggestive" in the freedom of the mind with which he unprepossessedly and insouciantly surveys and measures the sanctuary of his god? Our little theologian will read other theologians' books too, and from time to time he will find it necessary to "modify his position," perhaps quite radically. But he will never need to repent. For is not his god his to do with as he pleases? — For in the beginning was our little man, and he said: "Let there be a god!"

Or the theologian can make the choice that you, my dear brother, long ago have made. He can accept the God who has revealed Himself in all the uncompromised splendor, all the uncomfortable greatness of His Deity. He can accept, even though he cannot face, the terrible exalted holiness before which the seraphim veil their faces. He can accept the sublimity and the illimitable power that make man ask, "What is man that Thou are mindful of him?" He can accept His eternity, the "I am that I am," the one fixed point that will not flow with the flux of our changing thought or change with our mutable existence, that absoluteness that by an awesome paradox we both hotly desire and fiercely reject in the thinking of our flesh. He can accept the inscrutable wisdom that makes Him, in the course of this world and its history, the God that hideth Himself. But also he can and does accept with the inexorable hold of despair, with the clutch of a Spirit-wrought faith, the God of Israel, who came down, and drew nigh, and revealed Himself to men, and chose man, and loved him, and redeemed him — the God of Israel, the Savior. He can and does accept the measureless and immeasurable grace of the revealed God, the love past all searching out, the love of God that will not let him go.

Once that choice is made, once that complete reversal of mind and heart and will has taken place, then man, the true theologian, has become what our Lord here calls him — poor in spirit.

POOR IN SPIRIT

To be poor in spirit is something more basic than the virtue of humility. It means being a beggar before God. It means giving up once and for all any attempt on man's part to ascend to God, on moral ladders of merit, on mystical ladders of contemplation, or on intellectual ladders of speculation, or on any ladders whatsoever. It is to see steadily and clearly our own nothingness and the *allness* of God. To see that God comes to us, that we do not in any sense or by any method rise up to Him. It means living our life in terms of the second person singular, God — "Thou, O Lord, art in the midst of us" — and not in the first person singular of man ("I thank thee, God, that I am not as other men").

Being poor in spirit means, first, that we see God as the God whose wrath is revealed from heaven on *all* ungodliness (even on the idolatry that gives the subtle glory of being "humble" to man) and on all unrighteousness, as the God who in the inevitability of His holiness reacts to punish and to destroy all that is not holy and that is not good. But that is the beginning, not the end of being poor in spirit.

We see Him as the High and Lofty One that inhabiteth eternity, whose name is holy, who dwells in the high and holy place, but we see Him also as the God who dwells with him that is of a contrite and humble spirit, to revive the spirit of the humble and to revive the heart of the contrite ones. We see Him as the God of love, of that impossible, lost love that gave His only Son, His beloved Son for us, that we might find Him and have Him as the God that justifieth the ungodly; that we, who look upon ourselves in hopeless despair, might against hope believe in hope and stagger not at the promises of God. It means that we see Him, know Him, and adore Him as the God that hath chosen the foolish things of the world, the weak things, the base things, the things that are despised, yea, the things which are not — us — to bring to naught the things that are. We look back to His old revelation of Himself, and we see that He was from the beginning thus: He set His love upon Israel and chose Israel, not because they were more in number than any people; no, for they were the fewest of all people. We see Him as the God who deliberately took from Gideon thousands upon thousands of men, trimmed his forces from a mighty 32,000, a jagged rock of manpower to bash out adversaries' brains. He trimmed it down to a pitiful 300, a cinder to make an adversary's eye smart, no more, that He might say, "Arise, get thee down unto the host, for I have delivered it unto thine hand," that no flesh might glory before Him.

We come before Him with nothing in our hand, with nothing in ourselves — we bring our need before Him. We know that it is the God who commanded the light to shine out of *darkness* who hath shined in our hearts. In coming thus we give Him His proper glory as the Creator God, who creates *ex nihilo*.

That, my dear brother, has been and remains the nature of your life as a Christian, as a child of God, a self-emptied drawing upon the fullness of God, knowing that "God's grace and His kingdom with all virtues must come to us if we are to attain it. We can never come to Him. Just as Christ from heaven comes to us on earth and not we from earth ascended to Him in heaven" (Luther). In this spirit you pray that His kingdom may come, His will be done. You pray to a Father in heaven, asking Him to come down to you.

In this spirit you commune. The words "for you" are written not only in the service book but on your heart. You bring nothing; you accept God's gift from heaven, uncaused and undeserved grace.

> I hunger, and I thirst;
> Jesus, my Manna be.
> Let streams of living water burst
> Out of the rock for me.

In this spirit your works of love and mercy are done. In this spirit you become, in Luther's phrase, "a Christ to your neighbor."

And your attitude as theologian and teacher can be none other. For as a herald of God you can speak only of the God you have met and known, only of the Lord whom you serve, the Lord who has purchased and won you. Here, too, your prayer is, "Lord, open Thou my lips, that my mouth may show forth Thy praise." You are and remain, together with us all, a beggar before God. You know that "every ascent to the knowledge of God is perilous, except that which is made through the humility of Christ; for this is the Jacob's ladder on which the ascent must be made.

Nor is there any other way to the Father except through the Son." (Luther)

You know that you bring nothing to your task of interpreting Scripture for and with God's future workmen, nothing that God has not given you. It was God who separated you unto the Gospel, who so guided and shaped your course through school, college, seminary, university, and the holy ministry that you have come to serve His church here and now in this office into which you are about to be inducted. Your qualifications, innate and acquired, are a gift from Him, a sufficiency that He has bestowed and doth continually bestow. The rich and reverent exegetical tradition that you and I are privileged to inherit is His gift also. The parents and the home that molded you before you were aware of being molded, they too should not be forgotten in this hour; they too are from that same bounteous hand.

THE KINGDOM OF HEAVEN

We are poor; we are empty; but that poverty or that emptiness is our only possibility of becoming rich and full. For so, and only so, can the kingdom of heaven be ours, because so we are a clear and clean crystal chalice into which the cordial wine of God can be poured. He will not pour it into glasses that contain the dregs of self. But because we are poor, empty, beggars, hungerers and thirsters after righteousness, the kingdom of Heaven is ours. Upon us comes God's sovereign redemptive sway. Our empty hands are filled with His royal largesse, our hunger satisfied with bread from heaven, our thirst slaked by the water of life. The righteousness of God is revealed to the poor, from faith to faith. We have a king, the King of kings and Lord of lords, who redeems and saves, who makes all things new — us too. "Of His own will begat He us by the Word of truth. . . ."

Reborn, we have a new Lord, our Lord Jesus Christ, who has purchased and won us that we might be His own, His saints, and serve Him. For the Kingdom is given, not bought, acquired, or earned. It is called the kingdom of *heaven;* it comes from outside us and comes without us. The grace that there holds sway is the unconditionally sovereign grace of God. It comes to us and blesses us; more, it catches us up and makes us part of its great onward sweep through time and space. We are in that great resistless wave that gathers up God's elect, and we are part of it. We are part of it — because as selves — insistent on their right to exist, we have ceased to be. Because we are poor in spirit, therefore God can use us as instruments for His gracious will.

Because you, my dear brother, are a beggar before Him, therefore you can be a clean conduit for His grace, a clear channel through which the rivers of His peace may flow. Because you have renounced all egoistic working and acting, you have become a keen and useful tool, a trusty implement for God to use in His redemptive reign. Because you have seen God and believed in God as the God who commanded the light to shine out of *darkness,* therefore God hath shined in your heart and made of you a great reflector "to give the light of the knowledge of the glory of God in the face of Jesus Christ." And therein you are blessed .

BLESSED

Blessed you shall be in your work. That is as sure as God is true. Happiness you may have, and we all pray that you will have a full measure of it. But I should hesitate to assure you of it, as a theologian. The work is not easy; the hours are long — or what is worse, there are no hours. The problems and the responsibilities are grave. We shall find that the second Beatitude, which promises blessedness on them that mourn, was spoken to professors of theology too; grief is no rare vegetable in our diet. For we serve a church the glory of whose history is the fact that its course has always been a firm, determined confessional march; a church that never has had much taste for the mincing minuets of concession and compromise. Those mincing minuets are marvelous things to watch; they look so hard and yet they are so easy. But the hard thing is to march: to be good, not clever; to be faithful, not brilliant; to be honest, not urbane; to be the rough wool blanket that keeps the faithful people warm, not the flapping scarf of changeable silk that men admire. No one has promised us that confessing the truth will make us happy, but we shall be blessed — of this we may be sure.

Blessed, for we shall not march alone. When the communion of saints lifts up its united voice and prays, "Thy kingdom come," you will know that it is praying for you. When in thousands of churches men lift up holy hands and commend to God's care all our schools and pray Him to make them nurseries of useful knowledge and Christian virtues, they are praying for you.

We shall not march alone. We walk with angels all the way. God has given His angels charge over us to keep us in all our ways. And when we walk the way that builds God's kingdom we know that they are surely with us; for they are ministering spirits sent forth to minister for them who shall be heirs of salvation — for us, the poor in spirit. When we are faint and fail, they will bring the cup that strengthens and sustains.

We do not march alone, for He who sent His disciples into all the world to teach all nations has promised that He will be with us always. Grace and peace are ours from Him who is and who was and who is to come. His kingdom marches on. We march with that kingdom. His kingdom shall triumph, and we shall triumph with it. On that great day we shall shine as the stars forever and ever. Amid darkness we walk in light and toward light.

And the light that falls upon our present from that future, this blessedness, can irradiate all your work: not only those high moments when you walk on the mountaintops of God's Word, when with the prophets you see all heaven opened, look into the beating heart of God's redemptive purposes, and see the mystery and meaning of all history made clear in the long wisdom that shall sum up things in Christ. Not only there, but also in the drudgery and the detail, in the wearing minutiae of your work, this light can shine, this blessedness can be, as you, the poor spirit, the poor man that makes many rich, draw always upon the fullness of God, given, being given, and to be given in endless supply world without end. The droning drill of Hebrew grammar can be the figured bass to the song of seraphim, the needed foil to the soaring arabesques of angelic hallelujahs.

Such blessedness we wish you; this blessing we would give you, a blessing not our own but our Lord's. "Blessed are the poor in spirit, for theirs is the kingdom of heaven." Amen.

12

THANKSGIVING AND PRAYER

(Thanksgiving Day)

We always thank God, the Father of our Lord Jesus Christ, when we pray for you. — Colossians 1:3

We are the people of His pasture and the sheep of His hand. Why, then, do we give the appearance of being pastured on weeds? Why are we such worn and draggle-tailed sheep? Why is there so little gamboling on the green? Why is our life so drab? Perhaps, as our text suggests, it is because we have not learned the music of thanksgiving and petition, of praise and prayer. And they must be learned in that order, from thanksgiving to petition, because only living men can pray to God, and the people of God live, really live, only when they are thanking Him. He created us that we might be the firstfruits of His new creation; that we might show forth the praises of Him that called us. And we live, really live, as God's new creation only if we live in doxology, only in thanksgiving. And so we can pray and converse with this God of all giving only if we kneel upon a carpet of thanksgiving.

Luther once compared thanksgiving in prayer to the coals

in the censer. Unless there are the coals of thanksgiving under the incense of our prayer, it will not rise at all, or it will rise very sluggishly. But if there is thanksgiving there, then, he says, it goes up "fein lustig." And if our prayers are not "fein lustig," perhaps we had better take a good look into our censer and see what is wrong with the coals of our thanksgiving. I think that if we look honestly we will find that these coals are overlaid with layers of ash that damp those fires and keep our incense from rising in that "fein lustig," that jubilant and exuberant way in which God would like to see it rise.

What is wrong with our censer? There are three layers of ash we might talk about. You may have more, you may have less, but these three will serve. There are the layer of lurking paganism, the layer of the flattened-nose perspective, and the layer of preciosity.

The layer of lurking paganism gets in the way of our prayers. The old fear of the jealousy of the gods still lives in us. If things are good now, it can't last. If things are bad now, it had to come. If we have good weather in January, we will pay for it next June. If we have good weather in June, we will pay for it next January. We have had the Gospel a hundred years; we can't possibly have it another hundred years. Who said so? Certainly if we look at ourselves, our poor, weak, stumbling, fumbling selves, then the miracle is that we ever had it 10 minutes. But if we look at the good God, who is all good and only good, why should anyone ever despair of the second hundred years? If we have this lurking paganism, then we have a capricious God, haven't we? And who can thank a capricious God?

The second layer of ash lies on the coals a little heavier than this first one. It comes from the perspective of the flattened nose. It is this: If God gives us 99 percent good and 1 percent bad, we flatten our nose against that 1 percent. That is what we want to see; we delight in that 1 percent bad, and that is all we can see. We are like a man that has his nose stuck into a dish of ripe limburger — and the whole world stinks. There is this perversity of reborn man, this completely unnatural concentration on what God has not given us.

This sounds Pollyannish, perhaps. What happens to the good old existential *Angst* when we talk like this? We cannot, we should not, pretend that this battered caravanserai, whose portals are alternate night and day, that this poor limping and suffering aeon is our eternal, splendid, and delightful home, where God is All in all and we are with Him forever. But we should not, and we dare not, pretend that God has abandoned this poor, old inn of ours, that He has nothing to do with this inn. We dare not forget that He has entered into this inn, that He sent His Son to die in this battered caravanserai, that His Son died and cleared out of it the seven devils that haunted it, that we walk with feet of triumph in this inn. We should not forget either that the light of our Lord's return falls through the doorway of that inn and makes a path of gold to our feet where we sit weeping over our host's good wine. But if we have the perspective of the flattened nose, we cannot see this God, we cannot see this light — and you cannot thank a God you cannot see. We are like the princess in the fable. She had 20 mattresses under her, and under the 20th mattress was one dry pea. When they asked her how she slept, she said, "Terribly." One little pea under the 20 mattresses of God makes our whole life one sleepless night.

Then there is another layer, made of the very finest ash of all, a very select, choice product, the ash of preciosity. It is particularly an affliction of young men, and only one who has been a precious young man has the right to preach to young men about the precious young man. Your preacher qualifies. What is the precious young man? He walks six feet above the ground. His feet are tender, for he walks not on the ground but on the heads of men. He is a very superior product. He never gets his feet dirty, though he does not have very good traction either, and he doesn't get anywhere. Now what is the precious young man? We can picture it this way. God's waters come to earth dropping down from the heavens, gushing up in springs from the ground, in great rivers, washing in great billows upon our shore. They trickle and percolate through all manner of channels, sluices, aqueducts, pipes, conduits — come spurting out through all manner of faucets and spigots and unlikely apertures. But our precious young man thinks, and is firmly convinced, that it will flow only through his particular pipe.

That pipe has various models. We can touch only a few. You can supply the rest yourself. One of them is the antique model. It has a lovely patina of old age. The ancient liturgy, the primitive church, the ancient fathers! If it isn't old, it is no good, and God's waters can trickle only through this little antique pipe. This precious young man longs for the primitive church. He longs for the ancient fathers. Not too primitive, of course, because then he would be celebrating the Eucharist in somebody's dining room and would have a fruit cellar for a prayer chapel. But pretty primitive, back there.

Then there is the modern model, the chrome-plated model. It has to be recent. It has to be existential. It has to have the lemon astringency of our puny day. Anything before that just never was. The sun never rose until this young man saw it rise. Intellectual respectability is one of the highlights of this manner of pipe. Seventeenth-century Orthodoxy — ah!

Or there is the aesthetic pipe, preferred by the ecclesiastical gourmet for whom everything has to be just so. And of course water can flow only through that little aesthetic pipe of his. Well, there are other types too. There is the pipe of virility, the choice of the man who wants a he-man service, with the preacher cavorting like a Leviathan in the pulpit and everybody whooping and stomping it up. That is another type of preciosity.

There are all kinds of pipes. Understandably, very little water gets through these pipes. They are too selective for the God of all waters. And so our young man is wrapped up in fastidious discontent, and the sorry part of it — the desperate part of it — is that he enjoys this discontent. You actually cannot reach him. He is enclosed in the fortress of his preciosity, and there is only one narrow slit in it, and so he sees only one little piece of sky. Who wants to give God thanks for three drops of water? Who wants to thank God for one little, infinitesimal slit of sky? That is the tragedy of it.

Usually the young man grows older, and as he grows older, he grows up. And meanwhile God has His uses for him, as He has for everything else. The precious young man is a wonderful exercise in long-suffering and patience for all his elders, particularly for his teachers. But he is missing so much, and he is so slow in learning the music of thanksgiving! And sometimes he never learns it at all, and that is a real tragedy. Sometimes he doesn't grow up.

"Therefore," says Paul, "for this cause," "for this cause I pray for you." These words are a summons to repentance to all precious young men. For what cause? Paul has been giving thanks. He has been giving thanks for the church of Colossae and for Epaphras. There was not much to give thanks for. It was a simple little church, and the Colossian

Publishing House hadn't prepared them for the gnostic age. There was no literature. They were stumbling and fumbling when this thing hit them. Epaphras was a poor, faithful, little square-toed theologian who couldn't find his way through this. He had to go get help from Paul. But there was faith, there was love, and there was hope — these simple, homely things. And for these things Paul went down on the carpet of praise and thanksgiving, and for that reason Paul can pray, because he has eyes for God the King, who does these wondrous things in Colossae. And so Paul's prayers for us, for all us precious souls, all us men with lurking paganism in our souls, all us men that see the world from the flattened-nose perspective, are a call to repentance. Turn and really see this King, who created the earth and the sea and all that therein is, who created the church, who gave the heritage of 17th-century Orthodoxy, who gave us our fellow students and our teachers with faith and love and hope in their hearts, who gave us this sloping-floored chapel to sing his praises in, who gave us this poor preacher who stands before you — the one man in all the world whom God chose for just now to talk to you. Let's get down on our knees to thank God for him, whoever he may be, up here. Let's remember that Christ died for the many, not for a few. He died for us all. See the King where He is at work, here and now in our lives. If nothing blinds us to this, then we are ready to pray. "Large petitions with thee bring; thou art coming to a King." Amen.

13

THEOLOGY MUST SING

(Reformation)

Let the Word of Christ dwell in you richly in all wisdom, teaching and admonishing one another in psalms and hymns and spiritual songs, singing with grace in your hearts to the Lord.
COLOSSIANS 3:16

Theology is doxology. Theology must sing.

> The church with psalms must shout,
> No door can keep them out.

So at the Reformation, when the Word of Christ dwelt richly in men's hearts once more, when the peace of God was allowed to rule in men once more, there followed a burst of song almost without parallel in the history of the church. Here, too, the Reformation was not a revolution. It gave up nothing of the ancient song of the church that was good and profitable, and the Church of the Reformation ever since, when it has been true to its origin, has always welcomed each good new song.

But the history of the church's hymnody shows that the church has not always been true to its origin. The history of the church song is not an uninterrupted progress of triumph. So each generation of the church must try and test itself anew to see whether its song is true, to see whether its doxology is theology. St. Paul tells us that we are to teach and admonish one another with *spiritual* songs. If we can determine what "spiritual" means, we shall have the means of testing our song to see whether it be true.

"Spiritual" means wrought by the Holy Spirit, moved by Him, inspired by Him, coming from Him. The Holy Spirit is, first of all, a *holy* Spirit and speaks therefore with accents of His own, accents characteristic of Him and distinct from the world's. This does not mean that spiritual song does not use the words of men or sing the melodies of men. It does, but with a difference, just as the language of the New Testament speaks the common language of the common man and yet is no common speech. And so the church's song must speak with accents of its own, both in music and in text.

The Holy Spirit is the Firstfruits, the Earnest Money, the Seal of our heavenly inheritance. He is the Beginning and the Guarantee of heaven for us. A spiritual song must therefore breathe the air of eternity, must have a scent of heaven about it. It must be the prelude and the beginning of that new song which the church triumphant shall one day sing in the New Jerusalem.

The Holy Spirit is the confessor Spirit. "No man can say that Jesus is the Lord but by the Holy Ghost." If our songs are to be spiritual, they must confess; they must speak of the hope that is in us; they must tell of the mighty deeds of God in Christ in our behalf. Doxology, we say again, must be doctrinal: it must be theology.

The Holy Spirit is not a Spirit of slavery that slinks and cringes in fear. He is a Spirit of adoption and of sonship. Where this Spirit is, there is the free, confident atmosphere that exists between Father and child. Our songs must breathe that confidence, that sonship.

Where the Holy Spirit is, there is life, peace, and joy. There is life; we want no sluggish songs that crawl upon their belly and eat the dust. This peace is not a flat monotony of doing nothing, but the vibrant peace of a life of continual repentance, of continual renewal. And there is joy, that deep joy which is felt as the continued pulse of the church's life even in its most solemn moments of confession, humiliation, and prayer.

The Holy Spirit is a teaching Spirit, a Spirit that leads us into all truth. He is at the same time the Spirit that brings oneness and communion. Where this spirit works, there can be no such thing as a rampant self-asserting individualism, nor can there be a sentimental self-contemplating individualism. Where this Spirit is, there brethren know and feel themselves members one of another. They teach and admonish one another.

This Spirit is the Spirit of power. Our songs must soar:

> The heavens are not too high,
> His praise may thither fly.

The Spirit is at the same time the Spirit of love that condescends and suffers all things.

> The ground is not too low,
> His praises there may grow.

And He is the Spirit of a sound mind, so that we do not misuse the liberty which is wherever the Spirit is but welcome and exercise discipline, since we know by this Spirit's teaching that "God is not the Author of confusion but of peace."

As we survey the hymnody of the Reformation we can but gratefully acknowledge that God has here given the church a song that is really spiritual. And as we survey all hymnody we must acknowledge that the Holy Spirit worked not only in the Reformation but in all times and in all places in the one Christian and apostolic church, that in the best of what

Christian poets and Christian music makers have produced the church possesses so vast a store of the absolutely excellent that it need never stoop to substitutes.

And yet there has always been a terrible fascination in *Ersatz,* especially for a sick church, a church grown so languid that it cannot bear to live in the tension of the last days. And so we have, instead of the splendid picture of the church universal making a full-throated, joyful noise unto the Lord, the picture of the weary church sitting in a padded pew, weeping softly and elegantly into a lace handkerchief.

And the amazing thing is how eloquent men can grow in defense of this shoddy *Ersatz* hymnody. They begin by criticizing the good hymns as "hard to sing." One might ask in return, Why must a hymn be easy? Who has ever said that it should be easy? Look at that woodcut of Albrecht Duerer's where he depicts that scene from the Apocalypse in which those that came from the great tribulation, who have washed their robes in the blood of the Lamb, sing their heavenly song. Look at those faces, their intensity of concentration, faces almost contorted with the energy of their devotion, if you would know what singing with grace in your hearts to the Lord really means.

The fact that there is an amazing agreement on the part of hymnodists and musicians in all parts of the church as to what constitutes a good hymn counts for little with these critics. The hymnodists' passion for perfection is viewed with suspicion, as a sort of professional snobbery, and is usually countered with, "I don't know much about it, but I know what I like." That is really the ultimate in snobbery. To pit my piping, squeaking, little ego against all the good gifts that God has given His church! It is worse than snobbery; it is ingratitude. It is as though God had led us out into His great, wide world and shown us ripe, waving fields of grain and said to us, "Here is bread, and all for you." It is as though God had shown us all the cattle on a thousand hills and said to us, "Here is milk and cheese and butter and meat for you" and we then replied: "No, thanks! It is not to my taste. I'd rather go to a messy, dusty, fly-infested county fair and eat cotton candy."

Another argument might be called the "tin whistle" argument. Its essence is something like this: "After all, a man can make music on a tin whistle to the glory of God, and God will be pleased to hear it." True, true, true — if God has given him nothing but a tin whistle; but God has given us so infinitely much more. When He has given us all the instruments under heaven with which to sing His praises, then the tin whistle is no longer humility but a perverse sort of pride.

Perhaps the most insidious attack of all is the one that says:"Yes, these hymns are inferior, but we must use them as stepping-stones to something better. We must use them to train up the people for the solid food of our best hymnody." I am reminded here of a little poem on an artist who sold himself out, a poem that is not nearly as funny as it sounds:

> He found a formula for drawing comic rabbits,
> And the formula for drawing comic rabbits paid,
> But in the end he could not change the habits
> That the formula for drawing comic rabbits made.

We had better be careful about indulging in such condescensions, lest we too find the comic rabbits too powerful for us.

Rather let the Word of Christ dwell in us richly, and then we shall inevitably find, sing, and produce the best in song. We must produce. The song of the church must be an unending song. The church must cherish the best, but its song should not be a mere repetition of the song in the past. Then shall we sing with grace, with all the emphasis on God and a most unsentimental subordination of ourselves. We shall

sing to the Lord. With our song we shall guide one another
continually to the center and fountain of the Christian's life
and thus really teach and admonish one another. We shall
sing in our hearts; the whole man will sing. We shall see
then realized the ideal of all Christian song: the whole man
with all his powers, with all the skills and gifts that God
has bestowed upon him wholly bent on giving utterance to
the peace that rules within him, wholly given to the purpose
of letting the Word of Christ that dwells in him richly become articulate and audible through him to the upbuilding
of the church and the glory of God. Then shall our theology
be doxology. Then shall we sing with Mary: "My soul doth
magnify the Lord, and my spirit hath rejoiced in God, my
Savior. . . . For He that is mighty hath done to me great
things, and holy is His name." Amen.

14

FOLLOW ME
(Beginning of School Year)

And Jesus, walking by the sea of Galilee, saw two brethren, Simon, called Peter, and Andrew, his brother, casting a net into the sea; for they were fishers. And He saith unto them, Follow Me, and I will make you fishers of men. And they straightway left their nets and followed Him. And going on from thence, He saw other two brethren, James, the son of Zebedee, and John, his brother, in a ship with Zebedee, their father, mending their nets; and He called them. And they immediately left the ship and their father and followed Him.

MATTHEW 4:18-22

American travelers returning from Europe fall into two major classes. Class A are those who come back filled with the wonder and beauty of all they saw and heard and smelled and tasted, men who are enraptured with a world older and riper than ours, a world indelibly marked by the history that has passed over it, often delightful, always interesting. Class B are those that complain about the European plumbing. At the beginning of the school year there is a danger that all of us become the class B type, complaining about the fuss, the routine, and the irritation of the opening mechanics, which wear you down until you feel that you can't stand the sight of another mimeographed sheet of paper. All this is likely to blind us all to the glory of what is actually happening when this seminary opens again. We are liable to deafen our ears to the fact that what is happening as we begin our work as teachers and teach once more is that this call of our Lord, "Follow Me!" is being raised again — that call which has never ended, which has never died, which has been handed down through the apostolic Word through all the sinuous ramifications of history, so that it reaches us in all its pristine freshness, in all it Messianic power — the potent and persuasive promise of the grace of God which has appeared in Christ Jesus.

It is the grace of God that a call reaches us at all, that we are not left alone in our darkness and in our revolt, that God does not do to us that terrible thing which He has full right to do, that He does not "deliver us up." In the darkness His light shines, and in our blindness that light strikes us, and in our shut-in-ness His voice still reaches us. And then a call whose content is simply "Me"! "Follow *Me*." The elective grace of God is in that call. The initiative is all with Jesus and not with us. "I believe that I cannot by my own reason or strength believe in Jesus Christ, my Lord, or come to Him." It is nothing strange that Jesus, the Teacher, should be surrounded by disciples, that they should be in constant attendance upon Him. But that He should call them! That was against all the rules of discipleship in Judaism. These men did not select their rabbi. They were chosen by their Lord. "Ye have not chosen Me, but I have chosen you" is written over the whole discipleship of every disciple of the New Testament. Jesus created the Twelve (*epoiesen*, Mark says) that they might be with Him and that He might send them forth. It is not of him that willeth or runneth but of the grace of God, the God that showeth mercy. It is that love of God which does not find but *creates* its *diligible,* its lovable object, as Luther says. It is love to the loveless shown that they might lovely be.

And this calling grace which appears in these words "Follow Me" is the grace that gives. "Blessed," Jesus calls His disciples. That is the first word that Matthew has Jesus speak to His disciples as their Teacher, and this word "blessed" speaks never of what man has, what man does, or what man acquires, but of God's gift to man. It speaks not of man's doing but of God's giving. The gift of the kingdom — God in all His omnipotence and mercy is your King, not because you deserve Him or are fit subjects for Him but because you need Him. God is your Righteousness in Christ, not because you have any righteousness that qualifies you but because you hunger and thirst for Him. God will call you sons and will be your Father, not because you have filial qualifications but because without Him you are dead. God will let you see Him, He will open your purblind eyes, you will have the beatific vision, not because you deserve it but because you need it. "Freely ye have received," as a gift, Jesus told His disciples when He sent them out to proclaim the peace of God to men. He charged their words with the potency of that soundness and health that came into the world through Him. "Freely ye have received." With that you can seek the lost sheep of Israel.

Every question that the disciples have is answered from this center of God's giving, of the gift that came in the call. When Peter asked, "How often shall I forgive?" Jesus took him back to the first lesson, to opening day, and asked: "What happened to you? What happened to you when I called you? What happened to you when I let you sit at meat with Me? The kingdom of God became yours. God forgave you an insuperable debt. God wiped it out and set you free — and obviously He set you free for forgiving." Or when the question of greatness came up among the disciples, Jesus settled it, saying "It is not so among you, for the Son of Man came to *give* His life a ransom for many. The whole greatness of your existence is in giving, as it has its basis in receiving. That answers every one of your questions."

And at Easter this giving grace appears once more in all its splendor. What is the first word of the Lord to the men who could not watch one hour with Him? To all who forsook Him, fled, and left Him alone, who denied Him? "Tell My brethren; tell Peter." What they had shattered and destroyed, He restored and re-created. The communion that they had broken He gave them once more as His free gift. And He crowned and climaxed all this giving with the gift of the Holy Spirit, who was to glorify Him, who would not so much "make up His absence as complete His presence." The men of the New Testament are all filled with the wondrous sense of gratitude for this grace of God, which they heard first in that word "Follow Me!" "Of His fullness have we all received, and grace for grace."

This elective grace, this calling grace, this giving grace, is also revealing grace. "To you *it is given* to know the mystery of the kingdom of heaven." It is God's gift to the disciples that they can draw the line from the sower who went out to sow to Jesus of Nazareth, that they can see in Him the living, acting, royal reign of God's grace among men. That is given to them. That they do not share the lot of unbelieving Israel, that they are not hardened in unbelief, that is God's gift to them. It is *given* to them to know the Father's name as Christ spelled it out for them, to see the Father's countenance in the face of the Lord Jesus Christ.

Twelve little men stood on a hill near Caesarea Philippi, and they confessed Jesus as the Son of the living God. "Flesh and blood, Simon bar Jonah, has not revealed this to you. — Your human father cannot give it to you. This is the gift of God." Confession is a gift, a good thing for a confessional church and a confessional seminary to remember. It is God's pure giving to us that we can stand on any hill and say, "Thou art the Christ, the Son of the living God!"

And this is the grace which begets men again to a lively hope. We confess Him as the Son of the *living* God, who breaks into the world of our death and creates life. The gates of death will not hold those whom Christ calls from the grave. "Thy dead shall live!" and they shall live forever. For Christ *must* go to Jerusalem and *must* suffer many things and *must* be killed, but He *must* also rise again on the third day. The Christ, the Son of the living God, conquers the death which He endures. The grace and the call of Jesus is the grace of God which begets us again unto a lively hope by the resurrection of the dead.

Such is the potent promise of "Follow Me." The whole New Testament rings with the fulfillment of it, and the whole New Testament brings it to us as the living reality of God's presence among us. And the beginning of a school year simply means that call, "Follow Me!" with its potent, persuasive promise of the grace of God in Christ Jesus. Everyone of your courses has ultimately that as its content and its goal, by the common consent and will of every member of the faculty. — We have a feeble little academic joke in the faculty. The exegetical department boasts: "We are the most important, really the only department in the seminary. We are more practical than the practical department, more historical than the historical department, and we have a better system than the systematic department." I don't know why we keep trying that joke because it always blows up in our face. The other men solemnly agree with us. They agree that it is so; that, I think, is the glory of this seminary and the glory of our church.

It's an old academic sport, unless things have changed

since I was a student, that you sit down and shatter your school into bits and then remold it nearer to your heart's desire, and your church likewise. Well, God forbid that we should ever grow so weak that we can't stand self-criticism! But it's probably in place to warn against the placid poison of petulance. I can't help being reminded of the word of Rosalind to the country girl who was dissatisfied with her honest, truehearted country lover and wanted something a bit fancier. It might apply to us who sometimes think that our square-toed, simple theology is not quite fancy enough to suit us. She told that girl: "Down on thy knees, wench, and thank God fasting for a good man's love!" I think it behooves us all occasionally to get down on our knees and thank God fasting for a church and a seminary that wills concertedly and wills wholly that all these halls be always filled with that one word of our Lord: "Follow Me!" Amen.

15

THE MAN WHO WENT HOME
WITH ONLY A WORD IN HIS POCKET

So Jesus came again into Cana of Galilee, where He made the water wine. And there was a certain nobleman whose son was sick at Capernaum. When he heard that Jesus was come out of Judea into Galilee, he went unto Him and besought Him that He would come down and heal his son, for he was at the point of death. Then said Jesus unto him, Except ye see signs and wonders, ye will not believe. The nobleman saith unto Him, Sir, come down ere my child die. Jesus saith unto him, Go thy way; thy son liveth. And the man believed the word that Jesus had spoken unto him, and he went his way. And as he was now going down, his servants met him and told him, saying, Thy son liveth. Then enquired he of them the hour when he began to amend. And they said unto him, Yesterday at the seventh hour the fever left him. So the father knew that it was at the same hour in the which Jesus said unto him, Thy son liveth. And himself believed and his whole house. This is again the second miracle that Jesus did when He was come out of Judea into Galilee. — JOHN 4:46-54

The Jesus of this Gospel, at first hearing, chills all us romantics of faith. He looks at first glance like a hard man, a remote man, a stern man. How do we find our way to Him?

The father of the dying boy rides 27 kilometers over rough terrain from Capernaum to Cana to the Man who had turned water into wine, who gave joy freely. He comes himself when he might have sent a servant, and he comes with a plea: "Come down and heal my son; he is at the point of death."

What happens then? Jesus strangely enough treats him as a typical case, as a test case. He is typical of the Galileans: "Except you [all you Galileans] see signs and wonders, you will not believe." And Jesus gives him a lesson in religion, a one-sentence lecture on the theology of faith. This is cold water in the face of an agonized man.

And what happens then? The abashed agony of the father appears in his renewed plea. He does not talk about his *son* anymore. He says: "Come down ere my *child* die! My little boy, my love, my delight, my little, running, laughing, jumping boy, the light of my house, the hope of my life — he's lying there and every breath is an agony. That lecture on theology — oh, save that for later, come down *now* and heal him, my little boy!"

And what happens then? "Go thy way; thy son liveth." Jesus sends the man home with only a word in his pocket. Back he goes over the 27 kilometers. Perhaps a saddled beast that was to have carried the Healer to the boy's bedside trots along riderless beside him.

And what happens then? This is the unnoticed miracle in this miracle story. The man believed the words of Jesus, and he went his way.

What manner of Man is this, that not only winds and waves obey Him, but an agonized father of a dying boy picks his way home, across the ruins of his shattered hope, on a word alone? He believed; his was probably one of the minutest of the mustard seeds of faith. And no sign, no miracle — he had that word in his pocket, and that was all he had to go on for those 27 kilometers. But it is faith that sees signs and wonders. His servants meet him on the way with the good news, "Thy son liveth." This man at

Cana had spoken at the seventh hour, and at the seventh hour the deed was done.

This hard, remote Jesus, this stern Christ, has given this father more than he ever thought to ask. He has given him faith, a faith not tied to one need, a faith not tied to one sign, a faith that sees the Christ in His Word, and sees Him not as a means to an end but as the one great End, the one Pearl of great price; a faith that can find the whole Christ and live of this Christ in His Word; the kind of faith that does not remain bottled up under pressure like gas in a bottle (something that I can heat my water on for my cup of tea). This is a faith that controls the whole of life. This therefore is a faith that can move out and catch up others in its movement of adoration and gratitude: "Himself believed *and his whole house.*"

Dearly beloved, what shall we learn therefrom? as our father used to say. It is still a very good question. Two things at least:

1. Let us learn to look full upon the face of Christ, even when that face looks stern. It is always the face of Him who loved us and gave Himself for us. It is always the face of Him who died for us and rose again that we might never die again. There is more compassion in this Man's sternness, more real love than in all the bland beamings of the pseudo-Jesuses that men construct according to their heart's desires.

2. When Jesus sent this man home with only a word to go on, with only a word in his pocket, He was ministering mightily to us all. He shifted *our* faith from signs and wonders to His word.

Do we seek signs and wonders? Is not that an ancient vice? Do *we* have this vice, we who live in a universe governed by laws? We who walk down a road on which cause and effect, cause and effect, bump each other along like a string of docile idiots? Is this our fever? Do we suffer from this ancient disease of seeking signs and wonders? Are we not leery of them? Are we not embarrassed about them when they do happen or seem to happen? Are *we* sign seekers? Each man can speak only for himself. I think we do. I do. I remember a very stern word addressed to me in my sophomore year that I've never forgotten. It was by the president of my college. He said, "The trouble with you, Franzmann, is that you want everything 'high blue.' " And I did. I wanted everything "high blue" always. And we all do. We don't want to go these 27 kilometers with only a word in our pocket. We want a "lift"; we want a "motivation"; we want an "ecstasy"; we want to walk through a dreamy landscape or ride on a cushioned palfrey of emotions.

And that too, although we have a much richer Word, a much more fully articulated Word, a much more loaded Word, than the poor nobleman had to go on. What did he know about the Jesus, the Man who could turn water into wine? The wondrous Man of Cana, what do we know about Him? We have His Word as the Word of Him who was with God and is God. We have His Word as the Word of Him through whom all things came to be. We sing "The whole world is in Thy power, O Lord, King Almighty; there is no man that can gainsay Thee." We have the Word of Him who is Light, who is Light shining invincibly in darkness, who is the true Light. We have the Word of one who gives us power to become the sons of God; we have the Word that was made flesh and dwelt among us. We have the Word of Him for whose fullness we have all received, and grace for grace. We have the Word of Him who is the Grace and the Truth and the Fidelity of God in person. We have the Word of Him who is God's great Exegete, the

Speller-out of the invisible God to us in our needs. We have the Word of one who is the Lamb of God that takes away the sins of the world, the everlasting Son of God, the house of God, the Bethel upon which the angels of God descend. We have the Word of Him who is the Giver of wine to make glad the heart of man. We have the Word of the Son of man who was lifted up in the wilderness for the salvation of a mankind under the wrath of God. We have the Giver of living water; we have the Bringer and Revealer of true worship in Spirit and in truth; we have the Savior of the world.

"Hear ye Him! Hear ye Him!" — that was the climax of the transfiguration. "Go thy way," He tells us. Let us learn to go our way, let us learn to hear His Word in every fraction and every portion of our lives, including our professional lives, in the days when we are down, way down. Let us find the faith that this poor nobleman found, the veriest, tiniest mustard-seed faith, it may be, but *faith* that encloses the living power of God. Let us hear His word: "Thy work liveth; thy future liveth; thy vocation liveth; thy theology (thy poor, mangy little theology that seems all unintegrated), thy theology liveth! Thy poor, troubled, cramped, struggling faith liveth, thou livest, and thou shalt serve Me." Take Him at His word.

We all look for signs, even we sober exegetes. We are always looking for signs and are afraid to go by the Word. Emily Dickinson once said of poetry: "I don't know what poetry is, but when I read something and I feel as though the top of my head has been blown off, I know that's poetry." And I think the same thing can be said of revelation. Revelation is hard to define, but if we meet a revelatory word and we feel as though the top of our head has been blown off, then we know that is really God at work. But we always want our heads blown off right away; we won't wait, we won't go the 27 kilometers (and sometimes it is 54 kilometers and sometimes 108 kilometers) of weary, slugging dictionary-paging, concordance-thumbing work. We won't go the 27 kilometers; we want our heads blown off first. Let us learn to take this Man from Cana at His word, and go the 27 kilometers and not despair. We shall find that the top of our heads will be blown off by the strangest words in the strangest places.

> Made lowly wise, we pray no more
> For miracle and sign.
> Anoint our eyes to see within
> The common, the divine.
>
> Amen.